START the WORK

HOW TO DUPLICATE YOURSELF AND SCALE YOUR BUSINESS

NATALIE DAWSON

DEDICATION

To my husband - You are my greatest mentor and a business savant. Thank you for the lessons - I promise to be your best student. May we never stop chasing our potential and help others do the same.

CONTENTS

INTRODUCTION

Running a business and growing it are two different things. What holds business owners and leaders back from exponential growth is where they're spending their time. That's it. The truth is that while most leaders are in the trenches running their business, they are putting off the work that's going to help them scale and grow their team, reach, and revenue. To make things worse, they aren't aware of what the scaling process entails. Nobody ever told them. Everybody would like to scale their business, but what the heck does that look like? What specifically do you have to do?

As the co-Founder and President of Cardone Ventures, not only have I overseen the scaling of our business, I've also coached thousands of clients through the process of growing their revenue exponentially. I think it's important to be clear about the results of Cardone Ventures. After all, you should only seek advice from those who've done what you're trying to do. So let me hit you with some stats. My husband and I founded Cardone Ventures in partnership with Grant and Elena Cardone in June 2019. That year, we generated $2.7m in revenue. In 2020 we generated $14.4m, in 2021 we popped to $38.4m, 2022 wrapped at $82.8m and 2023 came in at $146.8m. Needless to say, we've grown. A lot!

For the first 2 years, I was head of people, operations, technology and we ran 40 events per year. Every day was a balancing act of different roles and, to be honest, I didn't particularly love any of them. But those roles didn't last forever. What I was once solely responsible for, today we have 220 team members doing. Incrementally, I've replaced myself with team leaders who excel in each role. This book is the culmination of all of my secrets on how I teach my teams and partner companies how to scale out of their roles. Learning to replace yourself with someone equal or better. This is the art of duplication and it's vital to create the business you want.

It's important you know our growth so you understand how quickly a business can excel with the right goals and founders who know how this game works. We practice what we preach, teaching it to tens of thousands of business owners who have created remarkable results by following our lead. Seeing common gaps in understanding and a lack of focus on the tactile processes that go hand-in-hand with scaling, I've written this book to give you the tools, practices, and outlook you need to lead the organizational and departmental shifts necessary for growth.

The result is a guide to duplicate what's already working, remove what isn't, and get you to the next iteration of your business. Done correctly, the process of scaling is cyclical. A business with a good core product should continue to grow when its leader remains true to the inherent principles of growth. It's a myth that your business should be stagnant or only see 5% growth year-over-year. Because of this, I invite you to use the following chapters as you would a handbook: reading through thoroughly the first time to find what's missing in your business today, executing and implementing those items, and then keeping it handy for your reference as new challenges arise.

The content of this book applies to every industry because growth hinges on the leader, not the specific business function. These are the proven tactics to shift your leadership away from what got your business started and into the headspace primed for growth.

The book is broken down into 4 distinct sections: *Time, You, Your Culture, Your Team.*

The first section, *Time*, is the foundation for the next 3 sections. In this section, I give you the scaling framework that should govern how you think about your time and where you should be spending it. The reality is this: there are more successful people in your industry than you. Why? They're spending their time differently than you. You both have the same 24 hours in a day. Time is the great equalizer. So you must understand how to use time to get to where you want to go instead of always feeling like there's never enough. In the *You, Your Culture*, and *Your Team* sections, I dive deep into the non-negotiables of where you need to be spending your time to create the growth you're looking for. The *You* section breaks down the personal habits, choices, and practices that I've studied across tens of thousands of business owners. Your business starts with you and where you spend your time and yet no one tells you what things matter and what things don't when you're starting and scaling your business. But don't you worry – I'm here to help. In *Your Culture*, we're going to explore the elements that are necessary for you to design a culture that scales. The culture applies to every department in a business. It's dictated by the values you put in place and the way information and data flow throughout your business. Finally, *Your Team* is the specific interactions and structure you should have in place with the individual team members who report to you. When done correctly, you will be able to stay focused on growing your business and adding additional revenue streams to your organization. The way you do this will determine how your team members duplicate themselves in your business which is ultimately the goal.

You didn't start your business so that you can have a job that you're chained to – with the additional responsibility of taking care of all your employees. If you're anything like the business owners I've worked with, you started your own business because you wanted to create a quality of life that allows you to do what you want, whenever you want. And yet, you've found that the opposite is your reality. You can't leave your business without your team constantly calling and texting about client problems and employee issues. It doesn't have to be like this. But you're going to need to spend intentional time learning how to duplicate yourself inside your business. I can promise it's not the most glamorous work, but once you've followed the process, you'll have created the business and the life you've always dreamed of. It's my mission to help you achieve your goals. So let's start the work!

*All the exclusive resources I mention in the book are ready for you to use, along with videos, tools, and extras that I couldn't share in this book, go to **StartTheWorkTools.com**.*

TIME

☑ **WHAT DO YOU WANT?**

☐ LET'S DUPLICATE YOU

☐ STOP

☐ CONTINUE/DELEGATE

☐ START

CHAPTER 1

WHAT DO YOU WANT?

WHAT DO YOU WANT OUT OF YOUR BUSINESS?

It's a simple question, but one that too many entrepreneurs I encounter are fuzzy on. If you picked up this book, it's obvious that you want to scale your organization. But if I put you on the spot and asked you, could you tell me what the desired result would look like? From the lifestyle you want to create, the number of employees you'll employ, the types of customers you want to delight, down to the annual revenue and profit targets, you have to be clear on why you are doing all this work. Why? Because getting there isn't going to be easy. This book is filled with tools, processes, and all the stuff that most aren't willing to invest time in. Hence why it's called *Start The Work*. It is going to take work.

You're likely already working hard. But if your business has been at the same revenue and profitability year after year, or worse declining, you're not working on the right things. Read that again.

You need to start working on the things that will get you to where you want to go. For most of you reading this, you have not even decided what you want from building your company.

The reality is most people give up and stay small because they've lost sight or belief in the life they want to live. They don't see how the vehicle they're driving will get them to where they want to go. There is nothing that brings me more joy than helping people get clear on your goals, actually believe they are possible, and pursue them with everything they've got until they create the life they want to live. This is my entire purpose for writing this book. Your goals are possible. If others have done what you want to do, I can assure you that you can too.

So the most helpful place to start is by getting clear on your Personal, Professional, and Financial goals. I've helped thousands of business owners establish their goals using this framework because it connects all aspects of their lives. You're likely driven by what you can accomplish professionally, but that's not the whole story. You also have relationships, health, and hobbies to consider. Ideally, you envision a life where your personal, professional, and financial goals all harmoniously align.

You spend time with the people you love creating unforgettable experiences. You've built a business that you're still challenged by because you have an amazing group of leaders that you're actively developing and helping reach their goals. All the while, you have the financial resources that you've always wanted. You can buy whatever you want and give generously. You can write the biggest check at every charity event and you're known as the person in your community who helps others and can be called on when the shit hits the fan. This is why you need to figure out how to scale your time so that you can scale your business. This life is available to you. This and more! Whatever your dreams are, I'm here to tell you that you can have them.

But you will never get there if you're not clear about what you want. Along the journey, there will be naysayers, roadblocks, problems, challenges, and no shortage of shit you didn't anticipate. These obstacles will break someone who isn't certain about why the hard work is worth it. So before I move into the tactics, you need to get clear on what you want. This goal-setting framework will help you put your goals into categories that break down the most important areas of your life so that you can get clear on your targets.

PPF FORM

PERSONAL GOALS

1 YEAR

3 YEARS

5 YEARS

PROFESSIONAL GOALS

1 YEAR

3 YEARS

5 YEARS

FINANCIAL GOALS

1 YEAR

3 YEARS

5 YEARS

Take the time to be thoughtful about these goals and stretch yourself past your comfort zone. You should have a gut-wrenching feeling when you look at these goals because they represent your potential. As a high achiever, it's okay to look at the list and feel like you haven't done enough. It's in acknowledging this and accepting it that you're setting yourself up to do something about it. And the doing starts with where you're spending your time. Before moving on to the next section, download the Personal, Professional, and Financial Goal activity as well at the SMART GOAL activity at ***StartTheWorkTools.com***.

TIME

- [x] WHAT DO YOU WANT?
- [x] **LET'S DUPLICATE YOU**
- [ ] STOP
- [ ] CONTINUE/DELEGATE
- [ ] START

CHAPTER 2

LET'S DUPLICATE YOU

Sean Stagnates feels like he's treading water. Sure, he owns a dental practice, which he always thought was his dream, but things are not growing the way they did at the start. His day often starts with his team waiting at his office door. Before he can even take his coat off, they're asking for his help and insight, as little can happen without Sean's presence. He spends the bulk of his day stuck doing the patient-facing work that made the business a success in the first place. Nobody can do it like he can, so this is where most of his time is spent. He ends his day a couple of hours later than he'd like to, after putting out the many fires that always seem to spring up during the afternoon.

Sean lives his life reacting to his schedule and is so busy maintaining the practices that made his business a reality that there is no room for his operation to scale. There's no structure or processes, just Sean running on a hamster wheel, wondering why nothing's changing or improving.

Sarah Scales, on the other hand, proactively laid the foundation for her business to expand. While Sean's calendar controls him, she views her packed schedule as a collaborator – the same way she views every member of her growing business. Sarah's dental practice started on the back of her reliable, meticulous, and stand-out service to patients – but it's been a while since she's been sticking periodontal probes into patients' mouths herself. She looks back on the hands-on work fondly, but she's made the conscious pivot to focus on scaling her operation. Knowing that people are central to scaling a business, she's learned how to efficiently and accurately duplicate herself: delegating key roles and tasks to her business' rising stars while maintaining the excellence that her long-time patients have come to expect.

In the time that she used to spend asking eleven-year-olds how often they floss, she now is developing new training material for incoming clinic managers, negotiating a potential buyout with a competitor looking to retire to Florida, and tracking the real estate market two towns over, with plans to open her next location.

Sean can't even begin to think about making moves like these. His schedule is rigid because if he wasn't around to do the things that started his business, revenue would plummet. He's tried in the past to delegate, so he could expand, but the experience left a sour taste in his mouth. All of his time training was wasted on a team member who didn't work out. The problem was that he delegated before he duplicated himself, effectively dropping all of his responsibilities on somebody's lap. Patients were let down, key organizational procedures were violated, and Sean had his cell phone blowing up with texts, emails, and calls until 11 pm. Today, he is spending his time doing the same things that he was a year ago and his revenue is the same too. Sean wants to scale his business, but he's stuck. He can only be in one place at a time because what he brings to the table is yet to be duplicated.

Sean is not alone in his frustration. His issues are similar to many of the clients who have sought my help in scaling their businesses effectively. If you've picked up this book, it's likely that you also can relate to his struggles: you're stuck and unsure of what the process of scaling looks like. Even if you do know what you should be doing, you may not have the time to start doing it. Therein lies the greatest ally of the business owner who's scaling, and the fiercest foe of the one who isn't: time.

In this book, the rest of the strategies for growth mean nothing if you can't clear your schedule and level up the value of you time. That, in a nutshell, is what scaling is: you delegating your current role so that you can go find a new one that takes your business to the next level, and then teaching your team to do the same. If you're feeling like Sean Stagnates when it comes to control over your calendar, we need to dive into the nitty-gritty of where you are spending your time.

If we were to consider your business' growth as a ladder, it's you – the business leader – who climbs to the next rung first. Before you can move up to that next level, you have to know that your current duties and responsibilities will be covered with the same certainty as when you were in direct control of them. If you're spending up to 80% of your time handling client-facing activities, with the remaining 20% going to the inevitable firefighting and problem-solving that every business leader deals with, it's a lack of duplication that's keeping revenue stagnant and limiting your ability to scale.

Sean Stagnates (who continues to tread water) and Sarah Scales (who's on the path to doubling, tripling, and even 10Xing her operation) have one thing in common: they have 24 hours in a day. The difference between the two is where they spend their time. What keeps many business owners from successfully duplicating themselves is the fact that they are flying by the seat of their pants and aren't intentional about how they're spending their time. Your results are directly related to where you spend your time. If you're unsatisfied with your results, spend your time differently. You want to multiply your revenue, yet the opposite is happening: things are declining, stagnant, or you're growing slower than you want to be. To get the process going and accelerate it, you must leverage your most sacred asset: your time. As you start the duplication process, I'm going to ask that you be vigilant about accounting for and auditing your time. This will not only highlight your key contributions that need to be duplicated but also reveal the time you're wasting.

As a business partner to Grant Cardone, I get to see firsthand how intentional he is about how he's spending his time, which you have to be if you're a self-made billionaire. Grant is resolute in where he is going, what he wants to do, and (most importantly) how he spends his time. He doesn't care if he's rude and isn't worried about upsetting or pissing people off. He won't sit through the entirety of your pitch out of obligation or put up with small-talk-wine-and-dine dinners that aren't going to help him hit his target. If it doesn't make sense for him to be in a room, he'll get up and walk out. He constantly reminds me of how intensely you should guard your time as the leader of a scaling business. You must start increasing the perceived value of the time you spend doing tasks, client work, and projects in your business.

Let's say you need professional-grade photos of your office and staff taken. When you're starting in business, you may think "Oh well, I can just learn how to do this." Figuring out how to make it happen yourself may seem like the better alternative to paying somebody $3,000 to do it for you. Ask yourself this: should you be trading time for money or money for time? You can always make more money, but it's very hard to scale the amount of time that you have in a day, month, year, and lifetime.

The time it's going to take you to learn composition, lighting, photo editing, and finally get everyone together to take photos is well worth $3,000 to buy back by letting a pro do it for you. The problem is many business owners don't see this immediately, because they are putting a low value on their time. Remember the goals you had from the previous chapter? 5 years from now, you won't be worried about a $3,000 photography bill!

ACTIVITIES	FREQUENCY	TIME SPENT (MINUTES)	TOTAL HOURS PER MONTH	IS THIS REVENUE GENERATING?	STOP, DELEGATE, CONTINUE, START	WHO WILL YOU DELGATE TO	PROCESS DOCUMENTATION
Review calendar from the past four weeks and document tasks you've completed. (Add photo of calendar for past four weeks HERE)	How often are you performing this task?	Enter time spent on the task in minutes. Ex. 60, 15 90, etc.	What is the total number of hours?	Does this activity directly increase your revenue?	See definitions above	List team member name here. If no one is available for delegation, list "New Hire"	List stage of processes documentation
Calling to get client feedback	MONTHLY	120	2	NO	STOP		NA
Reviewing Department SOPs	WEEKLY	30	2	NO	DELEGATE	Gabby	NOT STARTED
Recruitment	DAILY	30	11	NO	CONTINUE		NOT STARTED
Social Content - Four Promos Per Day	DAILY	15	5.5	YES	START		NOT STARTED
1:1 meetings	BI-WEEKLY	75	2.5	NO	START		NOT STARTED
Leadership Team Meeting	WEEKLY	60	4	NO	CONTINUE		NOT STARTED

When you look at your time, you remove the guesswork out of what's stopping your growth. It's not a riddle anymore: duplicating yourself and increasing the amount of revenue you're generating starts when you can focus your time on revenue-generating actions. It is that simple! The basis for a scaling business is a leader who is planning their schedule based on the moves that are adding to the bottom line and halting the ones that aren't. Let me introduce you to your new best friend:

I've used this Duplication Activity with every business owner we've partnered with and personally use this to scale out of roles inside our organization. It's a simple framework to document and then assess where you are spending your time. As you will see, using it will allow you to not just know where your time is going, but also categorize the impact it's having on your desire to scale your business.

Here's how this works: take a hard look at your calendar over the past 4 weeks. Under the Activities column, write down every activity that you spend 15 minutes or more doing. This is going to give you a picture of where you're currently spending your time. This can be eye-opening as you might realize that, although you say you want to grow your business, you're not spending more than a couple of hours per week doing growth-oriented activities. Next, you're going to add the frequency with which you do these activities and the total Time Spent in minutes. The next column does some fancy math in the downloadable version so that you can see the number of hours in a given 4-week period that you spend on each activity. Don't forget to grab the downloadable!

The next two columns are the game-changers as they establish the filters you need to look at your time through moving forward: do these activities generate revenue and should I Stop, Start, Continue, or Delegate them? These filters, used in tandem, bring into focus where you should be spending your time.

Target spending as much time generating revenue as you can. In the early days of your business, revenue generation likely looks like marketing and selling your products. As you grow, you being the best salesperson is a liability because your business can't function without you being a salesperson. This is when you would transition your Sales

Calls Activity from the Continue category to the Delegate category. I'm going to dive into the specific process for delegating in a later chapter because I have a tried-and-true method for training a new hire to become you. As you make it a habit to constantly look at where you're spending your time, you'll be continuously delegating what you're currently doing to someone else so that you have more time to do the next thing that your business needs you to do. You likely can't build out new products and services if you're spending 8 hours per day fielding sales calls. So as you look at where you're currently spending your time, here are the 4 categories you'll use to determine your next step with that activity:

STOP

If you use the Stop category, that means that you, and no one else in your business, will continue to do this activity. This could be cutting bait on a project that you're passionate about but isn't picking up traction. It can also look like removing unnecessary steps to the way you do other activities that add time but aren't proportionate to the value. We used to call every client before an event and do a 30-minute discovery. It helped us be prepared to know who was in the room and what their pain points were. Although this was nice to have, it didn't make any impact on the event or client experience. When we stopped doing it, our results didn't change, yet it saved us 45 hours per month. Challenge yourself on this as you might be doing things that you think add value but don't. Stopping something altogether gives you time to do what you should be doing better and add new revenue once you've scaled your current offerings.

DELEGATE

These are the activities that you're currently driving that someone else should be trained to take over so you can spend more time driving growth. You can't stop these altogether as they're a core function of your business – it's just not required that you do them. Delegating usually looks like adding the activity to someone currently in your business or hiring a new team member to take on the role. This solely depends on your current revenue per employee, more on that later.

CONTINUE

This list should be looked at as your job description. What's required of you in your role based on the size of your business? Have you ever thought about creating a job description for yourself? I'd strongly recommend it. This is the expectation of your function in your business. The activities you put in the Continue category should be in line with where you want your business to go – not where it is now.

START

Now your Starts aren't likely on your current list of activities because you aren't currently doing them. This list should be added to your activities and include where you need to start spending your time to create leverage and growth in your business. These are likely items you put off because you currently don't have the time to do them yet they are essential for your growth.

Moving forward, everything you do in your business should be run through this Stop, Delegate, Continue, and Start framework. This process of assessing how your time should be spent needs to become a rhythm as your organization grows. Deciding on the fly what tasks should be delegated will become second nature. Being familiar with this kind of thinking will give you a solid footing to stand on because you can start to make sense of where your business needs your time. You should be looking at every request, meeting, email, and project through this lens. Any given Tuesday morning might look like this:

- Drive to work (30 minutes)
- Weekly project meeting (45 minutes)
- White-board session with the marketing team (1 hour)
- Emails and texts (30 minutes)
- Lunch with a client (1 hour)
- Driving in traffic (20-30 minutes)

Let's take the Weekly Project as an example of how to use the Stop, Delegate, Continue, and Start framework. Take a good hard look at this forty-five-minute block in your day and ask:

- Is this meeting revenue generating?

- Am I required to drive to this meeting? If I'm not required, who can take notes to fill me in on Decisions and Next Steps? (I'll get into this more in Chapter 14)

- What could be a better use of my 45 minutes?

In the case of the Weekly Project Meeting, I would recommend that if your business is generating $10m+ annually, you are not the stakeholder as it's not your role to be driving organizational projects, tasks, and updates. Your team is in place to help you carry out an array of different organizational priorities but resist the urge to get sucked into every meeting to make every decision. This is a powerful lesson for any entrepreneur who hasn't duplicated themselves as you are likely unaware of how many non-revenue-generating initiatives you're taking on. All projects do not have equal importance to you – the ones driving revenue should be where you spend 80% of your time.

So moving forward, whatever the activity, task, or action, your new filtering mechanism should be: is this revenue generating? If it's not, give yourself an allotment of time, less than 20%, which you'll allow yourself to work on non-revenue-generating priorities and then stick to it. As you start this process, you'll likely need to give yourself a couple of weeks to reorganize your team and your time. I've worked with many entrepreneurs who go through this activity and realize they're spending 80% of their time on admin and non-scalable client work. It shouldn't be a surprise that their business isn't growing.

I give myself 1 hour per day working on non-revenue-generating activities (administrative work, emails, etc). When you set a target like this, you become hyper-vigilant about taking on tasks that aren't focused on growth. More importantly, it forces you to reset expectations with your team members about their roles, communication, and your organization's output.

The fact that something was a revenue generator last month doesn't keep it from the chopping block today. Remember: if your business isn't growing, you're not spending your time on the right problems. The landscape of your industry is constantly changing. Growing your business is only possible if you are flexible and ready to adapt. I am constantly editing and recommend that you do the same. This is one of my favorite quotes from Grant Cardone: *"Your assets become your liabilities"*. What once was an important initiative can soon turn into an anchor that's holding back your business's ability to scale. An important deal with a client could have been worth 50% of your revenue but now their demands are taking your product roadmap down a highly customized direction that doesn't benefit your long-term growth. When you first signed the deal, it was a major win and an asset to your business. But over time, it becomes a liability because you are dependent on them and not making decisions in alignment with your growth because you have to cater to the client. Yikes!

If you fail to regularly review your schedule, these shifts will go unnoticed and you'll get caught up in the motions of un-worthwhile tasks that hold you back. Letting go isn't easy – especially for things that you know used to work in the past. But this book isn't called Easy Work. It's time to take the Duplication Activity and open your calendar up for the upcoming week. What changes need to be made? Start The Work!

All the exclusive resources I mention in the book are ready for you to use, along with videos, tools, and extras that I couldn't share in this book, go to **StartTheWorkTools.com**.

TIME

- ☑ WHAT DO YOU WANT?
- ☑ LET'S DUPLICATE YOU
- ☑ **STOP**
- ☐ CONTINUE/DELEGATE
- ☐ START

CHAPTER 3

STOP

Gardening is just as much about plucking weeds as it is about planting flowers. The same is true about growing businesses. One of the first things you'll notice when you start organizing your schedule and categorizing your tasks is the blaring number of things that are not serving your business' bottom line. Let's free up space for you to implement the strategies, tools, and techniques you'll find in the rest of this book. None of us started our businesses to simply fill our day with a laundry list of things that generate zero revenue – but if you aren't paying attention to where your time is going, your schedule will soon be cluttered with meetings, procedures, and tasks that net absolutely nothing.

When you've assessed where you're currently spending your time and are now looking at laying out your schedule for the upcoming week, the lowest-hanging fruit is determining which activities you should altogether Stop doing. Cancel the meeting. Remove the block from your calendar. Don't binge-watch the latest season of Billions. If it's not getting you closer to where you want to go, don't do it. Ironically enough, I'm sitting in our Scottsdale office at 4:13 on a Sunday afternoon with a target of finishing 3 more chapters by day's end. My brother just walked into my office and asked if I wanted to see a movie we've been talking about for weeks. The obvious answer is yes – I want to go. However, I can't. Why? It's not getting me close to hitting my target. Instead of having dinner and watching a movie, I'll have 4 hours to write my book. This is the power of Stop. To get where you want to go, you will need to say no. There will be seasons when you have more time to do things you enjoy. But the reality is if you're focusing on your business during this season, saying no to time wasted is the fastest way to grow.

Here are two principles to consider when putting activities into Stop:

1. Where can you create time instantly?

2. How can you take less time doing what you need to do?

Let's unpack these.

WHERE CAN YOU CREATE TIME INSTANTLY?

If something is wasting your time, there is no use wasting even more time mulling over getting rid of it. When you are labeling Stops in your current schedule, be decisive. With the right data available to you, the things that are not netting your business any benefits will be clear right away. The longer you dwell on it, the more emotions will get involved.

Here's how data can make you more decisive. Imagine you go live on a social platform every Wednesday and you've been consistently doing this live show for the last year. It takes up an hour of your time weekly and despite having a lot of promise, you only have sporadic luck closing deals and the majority of them produce $0. It's time to get rid of it, right? Then, almost out of nowhere, you close a massive $20,000 deal during the last call before the project gets canned. Does that get this task out of the doghouse and into the Continue category?

Thinking emotionally, your head is going to be wrapped up in the negative feelings of going so long without success as well as the positive high of that big sale. As with anything, when we use emotions to help us make decisions, they end up being the wrong decision. My husband always reminds me, "The only emotion allowed in business is celebration". With data, we can overcome this and choose the best path forward with certainty. Hour-long sales call, occurring weekly, and running for the last year: that's 52 hours of your business' time bringing in a $20,000 sale. Let's say your profit margin is 50%, meaning that the total yield of those 52 hours is $10,000, or just over $190 an hour.

Are you doing all that work for $190 an hour? I think not. This immediately goes into the Stop category.

HOW CAN YOU TAKE LESS TIME?

I tell myself on stressful days "I create time". It's an immediate response I have to those feelings of having "too much to do" and "not enough time". This saying serves me because I can instantly assess what I need to spend less time on and prioritize the most important things. Your ability to create time comes from you spending less time doing certain things that you need to get done. For instance, you might have a full schedule of meetings that you can't entirely eliminate. But could you spend 10 minutes in the meeting instead of an hour and still accomplish the same thing? Usually, yes.

This is how you create time.

TIME

- [x] WHAT DO YOU WANT?
- [x] LET'S DUPLICATE YOU
- [x] STOP
- [x] **CONTINUE/DELEGATE**
- [ ] START

66/99

CHAPTER 4

CONTINUE / DELEGATE

Finish the book. That's been one of the most common phrases on my calendar for the last six months. I may already have one book under my belt, but that hasn't made the work on this one pass by any faster. There's no way around it: writing a book equals time.

I've been converting my ideas into teachable concepts, going back in time to share stories from my professional (and sometimes personal) life to support them, and typing them out over long Chipotle-takeout-fueled writing sessions (with many revisions and adjustments along the way).

Funny enough, this section is one of the final touches to the manuscript (believe it or not, books are rarely written from start to finish). My editor has been clamoring for me to finally send it to them – while I've been busy with other things these last couple of months. From where this book began as a blank document, to where it is today, I've at times questioned the importance of finishing and publishing this book. There have been challenges, upsets, and losses across our businesses. Certain things haven't

35

gone as planned and my attention has spanned hundreds of employees and thousands of clients. As I've been challenged in practicing what I preach as I wrote this book, I kept coming back to the two things a successful business owner should prioritize over everything else:

1) Getting known (which we'll touch on in Chapter 11)

2) Developing your team (which we'll touch on in the final section of the book)

This book, from the jump, was conceived to serve these two objectives. First, I want to help the business owners we serve get access to the data and tools they need to scale. Throughout this book, you're going to pick up information that will undoubtedly help you grow. When that happens, I hope that I've built enough rapport with you that you'll be interested in partnering with us so that we can come alongside you and 10X your business. Secondly, this book will also be used as a manual for our growing team to help them structure their work and implement what I'm teaching to make them effective and aligned with our philosophies. It'll be as if they've spent years working here (see how I'm duplicating myself?).

Looking at it this way, writing this book has been one of the most important tasks found on my calendar. Yet in both business and leadership, there is always something competing for your attention. The purpose of this chapter is to teach you how to Continue doing the tasks that make the best use of your time. By constantly reminding yourself about what's most valuable to your time, you'll avoid any doubts or distractions that take you away from reaching your goals (like mine to finally get this book to you).

On the other side of the coin, this chapter will also teach you how to *Delegate* activities that are still impactful in your business, yet don't require your hands-on attention. But before we can learn to Delegate, we should first focus on the tasks we have to hold onto ourselves – these are the *Continues* we highlight as we go through our Duplication Activity.

CONTINUES

The joy of reviewing your schedule – and finding how it's serving the growth of your business – comes in the identification of these Continue tasks. These projects and processes don't just generate revenue; they're also the ones that necessitate your leadership and presence to pull off successfully. A Continue could be something that requires your years of expertise, works through your carefully built and maintained network of industry connections, or simply relies on your presence to ensure a client that they've made the right choice to do business with you. In any case, these are the tasks that top your role's priorities – think of this as your job description.

Have you ever thought about your job description? Is it written down? As I've grown in my career, I am constantly holding a yardstick up to measure how I'm performing against my peers, I find these peers by doing my favorite thing in business: GTS. I love to "Google That Shit". If I'm the President of a $125m company, I can go to Google and search for Presidents who are making what I'm making. You should do the same. If you're taking home $500k as an owner of your business, try looking up roles (not in your area as this can be limiting) of other CEOs or Presidents who are making $500k per year.

This search should either validate your existing role or be a wake-up call about the up-leveled skills and expected output of others who are making similar money. Then look up CEOs who are making $1m per year. What is their job description? Let me tell you: there is certainly a difference in where time is spent between someone who is making $500k vs. $1m per year. Aren't you curious to know the difference? This is a helpful way to get clear on what you should be continuing to do in your business. No two jobs are the same, but it can be a helpful reference point.

When you audit and categorize your schedule to discover Continues, take it as a win. In these areas, you've identified your job description and are clear on your contribution. This will help you feel certain as you go through the day that you're focused on the right things and not just firefighting. These are the areas that your business needs your attention on today. As the boss, these top-priority tasks are being handled by you.

If you're trying to just maintain your business, these Continues are your best friend; if you want to create growth, however, you must learn the never-ending process of turning your Continues into Delegates.

TURNING CONTINUES INTO DELEGATES

Scaling your business means that your organization's top priorities will shift as you grow. It's a simple idea, but it's so often missed. If you are still doing the tasks that you were doing a year ago, your business has failed to expand. A company will not grow past its leader – so how can scaling happen if you are not leveling up into new tasks? The problem for many founders, entrepreneurs, and executives is not one of capability. It's not because of an unwillingness to learn new skills that most business leaders are held back. For the clients I work with, it's simply a matter of time and energy. You can't move to the next phase of your role as a leader because you are caught up in your Continues. Without realizing it, you may be trading future growth in exchange for what's working in the present.

To scale, you need to plan a healthy cycle of obsolescence around your current day-to-day operations as a leader. As I said earlier, the magic number is 6 months for the rate at which my business scales. From the initiatives that I ran this morning to the decisions I'm going to be making this afternoon – these have an expected lifetime of 182 days (or less) before they become the responsibility of somebody else. With this in mind, the business leader who can scale successfully is the one who knows how to Delegate.

HOW TO DELEGATE

The common assumption is that Delegating is a passive activity. Done correctly, it's anything but. You have to be active in bringing your team into the fold of your responsibilities – or else you will never be able to phase yourself out of them. The best delegators are the business leaders who view themselves as coaches. You were once a player, taking the field and putting in the hours to become highly effective in your position. But you're no longer just an individual trying to get better at your role. Now, the question you're trying to answer is how your ability can be duplicated to cover your part of the field.

You can't just tell those below you what to do once, pat yourself on the back, and turn on Netflix with "Delegate" crossed off your to-dos. It's all about investing the time, effort, and attention to properly impart the knowledge of the tasks to those taking them over. Otherwise, you're setting them (and by proxy, your business) up for failure. Somebody watching a football game might think that the quarterback can take it easy during a running play. All they're doing is handing off the ball to the running back. Anybody could do that, right? In reality, there's a whole lot that the quarterback still needs to be doing: reading the defense, dropping back with meticulous footwork, and extending out with perfect timing. The act of moving the football down the field is delegated, yes, but the quarterback still has a responsibility to the success of the play. This is where your head needs to be.

DOCUMENTING PROCESSES

The more care you put into Delegating on the front end of the process, the more effective you will be in the long term. For every role that I've fulfilled as Cardone Ventures has grown, I've documented detailed Standard Operating Procedures for the next person to take on the responsibility. These include step-by-step instructions, screenshots for navigating particular software, video explanations, and any other tidbits that I anticipate my team members needing. I'm going to make you an expert at creating documentation of your role in Chapter 6. You need to master this and then you will train your team to do the same so that they learn how to scale out of their roles as well.

My recommendation is that you start the process of documenting what you're doing while you're doing it – with all your Continues – before the need arises to Delegate. It's going to be easier to document everything as you are currently engrossed in the activity. The tips you provide will be more relevant and practical as a result. If you're feeling overwhelmed at the thought of a task like this and questioning if it's worth your time, think about it like this:

Would you rather?

A) Set aside time (at your convenience) to write down the solution to a common problem before it happens.

B) Get phone calls, texts, and emails (at your inconvenience) from anxious team members struggling with that problem.

The people who chose B don't do it purposely (they simply haven't gotten around to reading this book). But these are the business leaders who try to Delegate, put trust in their employees to figure things out, and find that trust broken when they inevitably don't. The reality is that you can – no matter how special you are – be duplicated. If you're having a difficult time believing me when I say that it's likely because you've been burned in the past by a failed attempt to Delegate. Part pride, part worry, part having realistic expectations, it's not easy to pass off the critical tasks that we've grown used to handling as the boss. It's true; nobody can do it like you. The first step to Delegation is shifting that to mean: nobody can do it like you, yet.

It's a matter of teaching your team to fish rather than feeding them. If you're the boss who has a hand in everything – with processes that remain a mystery – it will be impossible to duplicate you. But if you let people into not just what you do, but why you do it that way and how you do it, they actually will have the tools and resources they need to emulate you successfully.

Poof! Your greatest superpower becomes your leverage over time. You should have metrics that can go hand-in-hand with each documented process. If you have to be constantly looking over your successor's shoulder to ensure Delegation is going smoothly, are you really Delegating? The last thing you want to be is a helicopter boss (and your employees agree). But simply washing your hands of it and not checking in on results is an equally unwise way to go. We'll get into these metrics more in Chapter 16. For now, just start thinking about what these metrics could look like as you work through documenting the process of your current Continues so that you are ready to Delegate when the time inevitably comes.

It's worth noting that one of the roadblocks to Delegating is turnover. You spend countless hours training a new team member to be you and take over certain tasks, just for them to leave a few months later. This causes you to step back in and get frustrated about all of the time you wasted. Something to consider is why the person left. Likely, they didn't feel set up for success because you did weeks of brain-dumping without any real structure. No one wants to have to remember everything you said in the first few weeks of on-boarding – true leadership is making other people's success easy.

You're being a leader by organizing the processes and training to give your newest team member the best chances for success. In the last half of this book, I'm going to share the things you need to continue to do as the steward of your culture and developer of your team so that you don't experience turnover with the high performers who will help you take your business to its potential. For now, don't write off this documentation as I find it's the key to ensuring duplicable, scalable growth. Even if you experience turnover with the first couple of hires you make to duplicate you, your time spent creating processes wasn't for naught. The organization is better for it. You will find the right person and it will help them succeed. Sometimes Scaling takes a little bit of patience.

LETTING GO

It feels like I spend every day figuring out what I can Delegate. As I've become familiar with the process, it's not always easy. The toughest was removing my role as the person responsible for finding the talent in our business in addition to designing and executing their on-boarding process. I was simultaneously overjoyed and anxious when the time came to hire our first recruiter. I had hired all 50 of our initial team members for Cardone Ventures and it took hiring 88 to find the stabilized 50.

Every new person understood that I was the one who vetted them. I took care that every single one was goal-oriented and embodied our core values. I was worried that my predecessor would not have the same eye or that they would allow somebody in who was a wrong fit. Or even worse, they'd find great people and lose them in a poorly executed on-boarding process. Maybe that great talent would even share with their friends that the experience with our brand was terrible. You may share similar anxieties about giving away certain responsibilities. But, when you have a process and strategy in place around Delegation, what we fear most often turns out opposite to our expectations.

I found an amazing person to replace my recruitment function in our business, but I did not stop there. I was specific and careful of how I spent time with her and had her watch me during interviews. I had documented everything that I was doing in that role so that she could do it. Then, I gave her a healthy amount of wiggle room to improve those processes. Now, she kicks ass – and is better at the role than I was. I'm proud of that. When Delegating that's what the target should be. That can only happen when you can let go of control and give your team the wheel.

Sure, there were growing pains. When I was training her, I'd watch her ask questions, saying things like "Well, she's not doing it like I do it", or "Actually, I'd do it like that". This is human nature and one of the things that you'll have to get used to if you're ever going to Delegate effectively. Getting to the next level will require you to let people fill your role in their own way. You can set people up with your processes and training, but they are their own person and have their own flair. Embrace it.

A year into launching the business, there was a client on-boarding presentation that I was the best at and responsible for making. But it comes as no surprise that I reached a point when there was a better use of my time than consistently making this presentation, so I started training somebody else to do it. It was like nails on a chalkboard. He brought an entirely different energy than I used to and I couldn't get over that stark contrast. Despite all my hang-ups, the clients loved him. They would email me after his presentations to make sure I knew how amazing he was. This helped me understand a valuable lesson in Delegation: people learn from others in different ways. Just because I thought things weren't being done my way, doesn't mean that people weren't benefiting from it. These fresh perspectives – when balanced by diligent processes that impart your unique contributions to the role – make Delegating the powerful thing that it is.

THE CYCLE OF DELEGATION

If you're scaling sustainability, you are going to get familiar with the process of consciously turning Continues into Delegates. Just as yesterday's Continue is today's Delegate, the things you have started doing (based on the next chapter) will flow into Delegates soon enough. It's a cycle. As you grow, it won't be exclusive to you. The people that you Delegate to will one day pass that work on in the same manner you did. That's why understanding the recipe for a successful Delegation and having all these processes laid out is critical.

There are instruction books for roles that I have not fulfilled personally for years that are still being used in our business. There have been multiple team members who have come in to take on the responsibility since, and each has been set up for success by the details and resources provided. It's rare that I'm getting called for guidance on troubleshooting issues, or for my help in explaining how something should be done. That's because I used documentation as a means to duplicate myself. As the cycle suggests – the effort you put into Delegation in the short term only multiples in the long term. Developing the skill of recognizing Continues and turning them into Delegate is the name of the game when it comes to Scaling.

All the exclusive resources I mention in the book are ready for you to use, along with videos, tools, and extras that I couldn't share in this book, go to **StartTheWorkTools.com.**

TIME

- ☑ WHAT DO YOU WANT?
- ☑ LET'S DUPLICATE YOU
- ☑ STOP
- ☑ CONTINUE/DELEGATE
- ☑ **START**

CHAPTER 5

START

When you are running a business, you have a growing list of projects and tasks that you know are necessary to level up your operation. Lack of time is no longer an excuse – not after you've removed all the Stops from your schedule. In the void left behind in your calendar, Starts should be added and prioritized. And if you already know what you should be doing – get to it!

For example, many of my clients know that they should be making content around their business. Getting known is invaluable at all stages of your business growth and, as the person responsible for growing your business; this responsibility should be continuously prioritized. Yet, while the need to make content is apparent, so many business leaders put it off. If there are things like this that you are not getting around to, consider this your wake-up call. You can't simultaneously think "I want to grow my business and I'm going to do everything I can to make it a success" while not actually doing any activities that create the growth.

WHAT YOU DON'T KNOW

While there are things that you know you have to get around to Starting, there are also things missing from your schedule that you've never considered. You don't know what you don't know, so how can one figure out what they should be Starting in order to scale their business? The answer is found in looking at other business owners who are having success at your stated revenue target (if you don't know your revenue target, that's a problem. We'll fix that in Chapter 12).

If each level of growth is like the rungs on a ladder, you have to study what the next level up looks like, to start making it a reality in your day-to-day schedule. This can happen from a distance, by learning through the books, courses, and content of someone who's done what you're trying to do, or up close through a personal mentor willing to share how they created success.

In either case, it's better to hyperfocus on only a couple of sources to derive what you should be Starting. Trying to balance too many voices and opinions in developing the next stage of your business will make a Frankenstein's monster of your plans and muddle your vision. As with everything in business, collaboration is the name of the game. The relationships you can build with peers and individuals who are already accomplishing what you want out of your business will determine how high you can go. When you're figuring out what you need to Start doing to scale, remember that you don't know what you don't know so seeking out relationships and information that fill in that gap is the next best course of action. Don't overcomplicate this. Only seek information from people who have built what you're trying to build. Once you find the select few, go all in on their content and get as close as possible to learn from them about the specific skill you need to develop. I have to give my husband full credit on this as he's broken down the 3 questions you should ask anyone before taking their advice:

1) What's the most amount of money you've ever made in one year?

2) What's the biggest thing you've ever built (quantified revenue, profitability, and number of employees)?

3) What's the largest exit you've ever had as an owner/partner/or employee of a business?

STARTING TO SCALE

While the specifics will vary based on your industry and the level you are scaling from, moving up generally means Starting tasks that surround coaching your team and the discovery of new opportunities. For example, if you've chosen to stop attending client meetings, you'll likely have to Start holding regular meetings with your reps to review their metrics and measure client satisfaction. The activities that you Start implementing into your schedule are going to be hyper focused on the outcome of duplication. Why apply your skills to one sales call, when in the same time you can coach five reps to 5x your output?

When you are considering what tasks to Start doing, here are three useful questions:

- Will this activity help generate revenue/profit and growth for my organization to get to the next level?
- What is my target for this investment of my time?
- What do I need to learn to get to the next level?

The same-old-same-old will do nothing but stagnate your business. To counter this, everything you implement as a Start on your calendar should have a target for you to evaluate if it's working. Setting a target also helps you be mindful of what growth you're targeting. I've worked with many entrepreneurs who invest their time growing themselves but don't get their desired results because the growth was generic.

For instance, we've all met someone who has a target to read one book per week for the entire year. It's a great target if you're looking to build discipline – although you could do that many other ways. Their 6-8 hours per week could be much better spent learning a new skill like creating funnels for their business for 3 hours and then spending 3 hours implementing the reading by creating and testing a funnel. This would be a much better use of time. It's incredibly important to be specific on your

Starts. It shouldn't say "promoting my business." Instead, the new activity should be "posting 4 videos per day on TikTok and LinkedIn."

CONSTANT LEARNING

Just because the hands-on work that your business was built around is no longer a part of your personal schedule, doesn't mean you have to exclusively just be managing. This is where the discovery of new opportunities becomes a part of your new workflow. Think back to Sarah Scales, the allegorical business leader from Chapter 1. She's a dentist by trade and profession, yet in scaling her operation, she's had to develop skills in coaching, negotiation, and M&A. When you go out and start seeking advice from those in your industry about what Starts to implement, you may be surprised by what comes up. You may even feel daunted at the thought of having to learn something new – after already achieving mastery in the elements at the core of your current business.

Once you accept that scaling your business means that you will constantly be learning new things – the process gets exciting and even fun. Just as I advise you to constantly be editing your schedule to rule out Stops – you should be regularly revising your Starts as well. Starts quickly become mainstays in your routines that need to be filtered out as Stops (if they aren't getting results) or Continued until they can be Delegated. This is the cycle of constantly evolving into the leader your organization needs.

YOU

YOU

We've been laser focused on time in these last chapters. You're learning the value of your time as a business leader – and becoming more diligent in how you guard and protect that resource for the growth of your business. For the rest of this book, we're going to focus on where to spend that time. Just like with money, you have to spend it to make it.

If you have a particular end game in mind for where your entrepreneurial journey will take you, it likely revolves around creating time to spend with family, friends, and the hobbies you are passionate about. To get there, you have to invest the time that it takes to scale your business to a point where it can exist without your constant attention. Remember when we discussed the actions you will need to Start taking? The rest of the book revolves around these. Valuable time will be spent on You, Your Culture, and Your Team.

First, you need to focus on you. The business will never grow past its leader. If you can't optimize yourself, nothing great will follow. There's going to be some tough love in the coming chapters because optimizing yourself is going to take hard work, the development of disciplined habits, and difficult sacrifices. The awesome thing is this: once you create habits around each of the concepts in this upcoming section, these will scale beautifully with you. I don't care if you're running a lemonade stand on the corner or are at the helm of a publicly traded corporation – these routines are all tools for growth.

We have a business partner who we've been helping scale his business. During our time working together, he was unfortunately diagnosed with brain cancer. This took him out of his business for two months as he focused his attention on treatment, healing, and family. If he had received news like this prior to being mentored on how to optimize and duplicate himself, this would have meant the end for his business. Instead, he had already put in the work to scale himself and invest time into setting up processes and routines for scaling. This meant that his business was able to grow, even while he was away battling cancer.

Right now, for many of us, time is a gift. You can use it however you'd like. That's likely why you're able to set aside time to read this book and learn something new. The reality is that we won't always be so flexible with our time. I don't mean to be morbid, but you never know what is around the corner. We are called, as business owners and leaders who have a responsibility to the future of our team, clients, and family, to be proactive with the time we have. That starts by working inwardly and investing time into scaling yourself so that you can then invest in your culture and your team.

If you got hit by a bus tomorrow, could your business still function? If the answer is no, let's start spending time to protect against anything that might arise. How can you start putting a structure in place to show up in a consistent manner? How can you be clear that the intention is to become an example that your future team can look to and replicate? These are the questions we're going to explore.

Let's scale *you* – and try to have some fun along the way.

YOU

66 99

CHAPTER 6

SACRIFICES

We live in a world with never ending memes and cute quotes that send conflicting messages. We constantly scroll past posts proclaiming you need work-life balance, health is wealth, family comes first, and money doesn't make you happy. So it's easy to feel constantly pulled in different directions which leaves leaders feeling insecure. I really wrestled with this early in my twenties as I saw people talking about using your twenties to travel and experience the world while others said to put your head down and grind – because you can't reap rewards later in life if you don't work for them in your younger years. I was looking for clarity that could help me navigate this confusion. It wasn't until my late twenties that I found this clarity in one question that I now ask myself every day: Does my reality equal my potential?

For most of my life, the answer has been no. My reality hasn't equaled my potential. I wasn't giving my all. When I first started dating Brandon, I struggled the most with this. I was young and didn't have experience yet. My lack of experience, next to him, made me very insecure. I would sit at business dinners with clients and not say a word for hours because I didn't want to ask a dumb question or have them think I didn't know what I was talking about. The longer we dated, the worse it became and my insecurity was especially pronounced when we would travel. I didn't have the skills, yet, that were commensurate with the lifestyle I was living.

I'll never forget traveling across the world to Rome when I was 24 to go on a charity trip with 50 other couples. It was the second time I had flown on a private jet and the entire experience was overwhelming. The cost of the event was more than I made in a year and the people were so fabulous and cultured. The first night they hosted a cocktail party to kick off the event. While Brandon knew people already, I knew no one and was intimidated and anxious. Why? All night long, we met new people and within the first 90 seconds, they would ask "What do you do?" and I didn't have a response. I work for his company? I'm his girlfriend? I'm 24 years old and still figuring it out? We ended the night hours later. When I got to the room I started sobbing. I felt defeated and not good enough.

My mom taught me growing up that "Things are always better in the morning". So I woke up the next day and took a walk around the grounds of the hotel. As I walked, I told myself that I was going to make a change. Instead of being defeated, I decided to suck it up because next year at this event, I would have a story to tell and interesting things to contribute. This decision instantly freed me to enjoy the rest of the trip. I look back on those 5 days now and wish I could relive it all knowing what I know today.

Leaving Rome that September, I made it my mission to put the work in to get the confidence I wanted. It was my "burn the ships" moment. At the time, I really let it sink in that if I didn't figure this out, I was going down a path that I would struggle to backtrack. I imagined what it would be like to spend the rest of my life in my husband's shadow, following him around the world, being financially dependent on him, and feeling this deep sense of insecurity.

I get that works for some people and they find fulfillment and true contentment – that is their potential. But there was this overwhelming feeling I had of disappointing myself because I knew that I was meant for more. I knew that I had dreams and ambitions that I needed to pursue. I didn't want to live a life where I copped out of all of the amazing things I was capable of. And the charity event I was at was a forceful reminder of that – I didn't feel like the successful people I was around were any different from me. There was nothing uniquely special about them – they just worked harder and didn't stop themselves from doing great things.

I'm sure you've had a similar moment. Maybe yours came from something more inspirational and less painful. I find that people are motivated by different things. Regardless of the source, you're reading this because you've made a conscious decision not to live an average life. You know you're destined for greatness. What comes with that is sacrifice. And as someone who has navigated this (imperfectly I might add), here are some of the areas where you'll need to make sacrifices.

It's important for me to share that I do believe you can have it all, but it might not all be at the same time.

FAMILY

Let's just rip the band-aid off. This is an unpopular opinion but I work with countless business owners who struggle the most with getting their family members on board with their goals and dreams. Building something great with your business means that there will be dinners and special moments missed. It's the reality and you get to decide to what extent. I don't have children so I can't comment on the struggle parents go through when trying to navigate being an involved parent with big professional aspirations. What I do see is TV and movies vilifying parents who prioritize work over their families. I had 2 working parents and am thankful for the examples they set for me of hard work and tenacity. I've also watched Grant and Elena Cardone set an amazing example of how to be an active parent while not using their kids as an excuse for why they can't do something for their business. They include the kids, take them with them on trips, and put them to work. They also explain to the kids that the mission of their family is to help people. The kids play an important role in helping their parents fulfill that mission - they aid in your expansion.

Family extends beyond children and you can find resistance from your parents, spouse, siblings, and others. Snide comments like "You're never around anymore" or "You don't make time for me" can leave many leaders carrying guilt about how much they work. It's important to acknowledge and explain why your work is so important to you – especially if it didn't used to be. Giving your loved ones the opportunity to understand is always the first step. But if it doesn't get through, let that shit go. This is your life and you are doing what you feel needs to be done to live it to the fullest. Sometimes the hardest people to change are family. Don't be upset. It's okay and this is normal. Love them for the comfort and beautiful times you do share and just stay focused on where you're going. You don't need to have them onboard to go where you want to go. Sure – it would be nice to have the people closest to you be supportive but it's not a necessity. Only you will live with the regret you'll have if you give in or placate.

FRIENDS

If your friends don't support you, they're not your friends. Unlike family, you choose to put these people in your life. Elena Cardone shares the most beautiful definition of support: active interest in the success of. If someone is your friend and supposed to support you, are they showing an active interest in your success? If not, move on.

After I came home from Rome, I decided to launch a blog. It was my first foray into the digital marketing world where I was learning about how to run a website, grow my subscriber count, acquire readers, and build my brand. At the time, I didn't feel confident talking about business experience because I was 24 years old and didn't have a successful business track record. Most of my experiences at that point were such big failures that I actually wanted to distract people from them. In an effort to find a topic I could talk about, I decided to create a blog called *He's 25 Years Older*.

Hear me out: most of the women I was friends with had large age differences between them and their husbands and there was nothing in the marketplace speaking to them. I wanted to bring light and resources to all of these hidden conversations I was having about step-kids, pre-nups, judgment, and fear of death. I was on a road trip with my college girlfriends, who were not dating older men, and I told them about this blog I was launching. It was met with silence and blank stares. One of them finally broke the silence by asking if they would "really have to tag the @hes25yearsolder account in photos moving forward…" I was crushed. I kept it together until I got home and, once again, burst into tears when I told Brandon about their response.

Luckily, they didn't stop me, but I wish someone would have told me the definition of support back then. The correct response from your friends to your goals should be "That's awesome! How can we help?" Anything short of that, you're wasting your time. I don't care how long you've known them or what history you have. They can certainly come around in the future and you don't have to have some big, dramatic separation. But you equally don't have to subject yourself to people who aren't in your corner.

HEALTH

You do not have to sacrifice your health for your business pursuits. This is a myth and it's an easy scapegoat for choosing to live an unhealthy lifestyle. Getting in the gym 4-5 days per week for 45 minutes is not going to be the reason that you didn't increase your revenue by 120% this year. I would argue that you will be able to do more and feel better, leading to increased productivity, when you prioritize your health. Sure, it takes discipline and extra planning but what you gain is confidence. I know that I feel like shit if I'm not eating well and regularly exercising. Feeling great in my body helps me show up in a stronger, more authoritative manner.

My thought process is that if I know I want to look and feel good, I need to do what it takes to make that happen. But if I don't do those things, I can make up reasons why. "I was busy" or "I was traveling" or "There were no healthy food options" are lies I can tell myself, but I'm not in the habit of believing my own bullshit. If I am not holding myself highly accountable in this area, I stop holding others accountable – which is one of the worst leadership qualities. High accountability = results. So if I know that, my health can't take a backseat to my professional goals because they're interconnected. Your personal life and your professional life are both your life. You're not two different people. So if you've listened to your own excuses and you've had enough, make the commitment to reprioritize your health. The poor decisions you made yesterday, or even right before you opened this book, don't dictate the rest of your day, week, month, year, or decade.

GOOD OPPORTUNITIES

When you are committed to your business, you will find that as you start having success more doors will open for you. There will be new opportunities that come your way because you've demonstrated that you're able to take an idea and execute. New opportunities are drawn to people who know how to execute. So here's a piece of advice, say no to the good opportunities that aren't your opportunities. Stay focused on what you're doing. Your Mission and Vision should be used to guide you in the right direction. If it's outside the scope of your services in an entirely disconnected industry, say no. And say no, knowing that someone else will likely make good money off of it. That's okay. You will move faster and have confidence when you stick with what is working and finish what you started. The greatest danger I see with business owners is when they start to achieve a little bit of success. They've duplicated themselves in their business to where they have more free time – they've created the life they thought they wanted and fought hard for – only to get distracted. Make what you're doing now bigger and double down on investing in the resources and infrastructure necessary to make that vehicle indestructible. If your current business isn't producing $10m in EBITDA without you touching it, you still have work to do. Stay the course.

HAPPINESS

I don't want to sell achieving your goals and dreams as if the road to get there is lined with lollipops and rainbows. You are going to have to learn things you hate and do things you don't want to do – daily. This idea of pursuing your passion and happiness has many people confused and chasing all the wrong things. Happiness isn't the target – your potential is. Were you able to make the impact you were meant to make? If not, you shouldn't be happy. Get back to work. I'm all for people having fun and living a fulfilled life but if your target is happiness, go pick up a different book because I'm not here to help you chase some illusive feeling. I want to help you become the person you need to be to make your unique impact on the world. I choose to believe that the people who have changed the world didn't do it to be happy and they likely were not happy along the way. Most success stories include despair, hardship, and constant pushback. So let's not delude ourselves – happiness is nice but not the target.

I know, I know – this is pretty doom and gloom. But here's the deal: no one can take your wins away from you.

Only you can assess your potential. It's not for someone else to judge, decide, or have an opinion about. It's for you to determine. I know when I'm capable of more. There is nothing you can buy or stumble into that replaces the confidence you gain when you've worked hard for something and you saw it through, despite the obstacles, to achieve your target. I would give everything up to keep the confidence I've gained over the past 5 years. I will never be the girl who walks into a room insecure and fearful because I have stats in areas that make me believe in myself. That gets created when you Start The Work.

Let's be real here, without control of your time, without knowing what to Start, Continue, Delegate, and Stop when it comes to your health, happiness, and your relationships, you're stuck in the hamster wheel of life. Only you can take control and choose to live into your full potential. I'm rooting for you.

YOU

CHAPTER 7

LET'S MAKE PROCESS SEXY

Let's be honest. The last thing you want to make time for while you're growing your business is documenting processes. It seems so unnecessary for a variety of reasons. You don't have time. You already know how to do what you're doing. You don't have someone to help you so it sounds like more work. And you know that you remember all the steps involved so what's the use in writing everything down?

As we discussed earlier, you no longer get to be this selfish. Documenting your processes isn't for you. It's for your team. Your business can scale to the extent that you master "the documenting your process" game. The art of scaling is duplicating the things you do that work so that you no longer have to do them. The challenge is that you don't know how and you aren't making it a priority.

Running a business can be a daunting task, especially when it comes to building processes. It can be hard to know where to start, especially if you don't have any processes in place. Why are processes so important? One of the main reasons for having them is to ensure consistency in your business. Without processes, it's easy for things to slip through the cracks, and for tasks to be done in different ways by different people. This can lead to confusion and mistakes, which can ultimately harm your business and lead to an inconsistent customer experience. By having processes in place, everyone knows what needs to be done and how it should be done. Not having processes is inefficient. More often than not, there is an optimal or best way to complete a task. If you aren't ensuring everyone is completing a task in a specific way, you're leaving the door open for people to invent less-than-optimal ways of doing things. This guarantees that time and resources go to waste and keeps your team from being as productive as they could be.

People are fallible. Especially when it comes to tasks that are repetitive or particularly technical. Processes are the guidelines your team will use to understand how to do their job, the effort you put into making them clear will directly translate into the final performance of the job. This is going to boost engagement and morale, too. Nobody shows up eagerly to a job where they don't know what is expected from them. Give people the resources they need to be successful.

There will be chaos in your business as you grow. Things won't always go as planned, but having underlying processes allows you and your team to at least approach change and sudden problems with two feet on solid ground. At scale, people are not going to be able to go find you to explain every little thing. Good processes allow you to be in many places at one time: your team won't need to track you down because you've answered their questions already in the processes you've created.

That ties into another difficulty that plagues teams lacking processes: poor communication. If everyone has their own way of expressing instructions, sending emails, or even different slang for the services you offer, you may as well have office space in the tower of Babel. Just like with language, the standardization that comes with processes keeps everything crystal clear. That garbage bin in your office: whose job is it to empty it? Let's say a process was never set, but one mindful and caring team member simply takes out the bag every time it's full. Nobody knows who's doing it, but it always gets done, so nobody thinks about it. Then that employee leaves and a week later, garbage is piling up. This is a silly example, but I see this with business owners all the time. They haven't made processes and can barely determine who is responsible for specific tasks or decisions. This adds to the confusion and also allows everyone on the team to avoid accountability.

On the idea of accountability, measuring performance is difficult, if not impossible, when you don't have processes. The process is what you'll use to drive the metrics you've targeted, so one can't exist without the other. All of these challenges that come when you lack processes will boil down to one thing: your business can't grow past you.

Before moving on, I want you to go back to your Duplication Activity and identify the specific items you marked as "Delegate."

Go on. Open it up. I'll wait.

Okay – now that you know the list of items you need to Delegate, this becomes our project plan for process documentation.

Let's pretend that this is your list of "Delegates":

- HR (i.e. Policy updates, PTO approvals, new team training) - 2 hours per week

- Marketing touch base/meetings - 2 hours per week

- Dealing with escalated client issues - 6 hours per week

- Running sales meetings - 2.5 hours per week

My first step is to convert the item I'm Delegating into a proper name that I can create a process around. As an example, I would never write a process called "Dealing with escalated client issues". You would never train your team to "deal" with client "issues".

This would need to be broken down into specifics such as: "Overcoming Client Objections Process" and

"Navigating Client Service Complaints Process". See what I did there? I bucket the "issues" into 2 categories: "Service Complaints" and "Objections". These are two distinct things that you're likely doing when "Dealing with escalated client issues" and your team needs to be trained on both types of issues. As a rule of thumb, most items that you Delegate have anywhere from 2-5 processes that need to be broken out.

After your list of "Delegates" gets turned into a list of processes, it's time to prioritize this list. In an ideal scene, you spend a Saturday for 4 hours knocking all of it out at once. That's my strong recommendation. However, I've worked with thousands of clients on this and they rarely heed this advice so I'll share with you what I share with them as it relates to prioritization.

If I were responsible for determining how to prioritize this list, I would look at a few things:

- What is taking the most time?
- How much effort will it take for me to document and train someone on this?
- Who do I currently have in the organization to take on this responsibility?

When looking at your Delegate list, it might seem like the obvious choice to start with documenting the "Dealing with escalated client issues". It's taking up to 6 hours, so logic would state that I should knock that out first.

However, if you don't have someone in place who can take this on for 2 months, it is not the best use of your time today. There are higher-value things that you could be doing. Equally, it might take you 6+ hours to document this because you've never really paid attention to what you say on these calls or bucketed the types of issues you're handling.

In this case, knowing that you're targeting to bring someone on in 2 months who will be responsible for this, I would spend the next month recording all of my client calls and tracking each issue and your response to them while they're happening. For every complaint or objection that comes up, you document what it was and then document how you responded. Now, if the client didn't respond well, I might not keep your response as something you will train someone on. Why? You're not sure it worked! Only document what you know works. When you do have a slam dunk response, make sure to list it but also attach the recording to your tracker. That way, you can have your new team member listen to 10+ of your calls on their first week so that they know exactly what to say and when.

SOPS FOR EVERYONE!

The more formal way to document this is in a Standard Operating Procedure (SOP for short). I'd like to walk you through my tried-and-true SOP Template components so that you can simply copy and paste this into your business. Don't forget to grab the downloadable to get access to the digital version of the SOP Template. It follows a framework called VCE: Vision, Commitment, and Execution. When people document processes, they struggle with communicating the context and purpose of the process. Keep in mind this happens all the time in business, particularly because people are moving fast, they're under pressure, and they're trying to get as many things done as possible. Bad process documentation happens when someone dives straight into the execution steps. Starting a process with a list of steps doesn't create the bigger picture of the importance of the process. So instead of starting with the steps, I recommend you start with the Vision for the process.

SOP VISUAL

PROCESS NAME	
VISION:	
COMMITMENT:	
EXECUTION:	See steps below.
TEMPLATES AND RESOURCES:	
VIDEO OVERVIEW:	
SCREENSHOTS:	PROCESS STEPS: 1. 2. 3. 4. 5.

Created By:	
Approved By:	
Date Approved:	

CHANGE TRACKER		
DATE CHANGED	WHO MADE THE CHANGE	WHAT WAS CHANGED (HIGH LEVEL)

VISION

The Vision category is the big picture of what the process is trying to accomplish. It shares with the team member that the work they're being trained on is deeply connected to something that is important to help internal or external stakeholders fulfill the Mission of the business. There's no such thing as "just a task" in business. Everything matters, even seemingly mundane things. For our example of Overcoming Client Objections Process, the Vision statement might read: "The vision for overcoming client objections is to instill confidence and certainty with every client and prospective client that we can help them achieve their goals". It's straightforward and clear.

You can find the full Overcoming Client Objections SOP at StartTheWorkTools.com.

COMMITMENT

The Commitment category highlights what you're asking from the team member in order to achieve the smooth execution of the process. It's to ensure that they're clear on doing the things necessary to help the department and organization achieve the overall goals. For our example, the Commitment would be "Team member is committed to thoroughly understanding the scripts within the process and duplicating them when overcoming objections with clients".

As a side note, this helps get your team aligned. Not only are they supposed to know these steps, they're supposed to use and implement them. I can tell you with certainty that as you add more people to your organization, they will start to want to do things a "new", "different", and "better" way. They don't get to start improving things until they've demonstrated that they can duplicate and master what already works. And remember you know it works because you were the one who did it that way originally. You used your calls with your clients to create these processes. You didn't hire someone to reinvent your perfectly round wheel. You hired them to duplicate you first. If you don't enforce the duplication step, you will create chaos in your business. Make this a priority.

EXECUTION

The Execution is the straightforward blocking and tackling for what needs to get done. It is the step-by-step plan for accomplishing the Vision. It's the "who, what, when, where, and how" plan. When breaking down Execution steps, I find it helpful to categorize these steps into "Pre, During, and Post". What needs to happen before, during, and after to ensure an optimal result? It's normal to prioritize the "during" phase and that's where most inexperienced documenters start. But take a step back and ask yourself, what do I need to do before I get on the phone with the customer? Ahhh. Lots of things such as checking the CRM for the last time the client was talked to, and researching the client to ensure you know the business name, first and last name, and where they're located. Those things are all considered "Pre" steps. The "During" is the script, set of questions, presentation, etc. The "Post" should include updating the CRM, emailing the customer within 10 minutes to ensure prompt follow-up, proactively updating the team if a timeline shifted, etc. The gold is in the Pre and Post steps. Train yourself (and your team) to pay attention and document all of the little steps that create value in the process. No detail should be overlooked – imparting everything that makes you great into documentation is the highest valued time you can spend. Don't do it half-assed.

TEMPLATES AND RESOURCES

This is a place in your SOP for you to add links to supplemental documentation that is associated with the process such as email templates, presentations, spreadsheets, or FAQs. All information that the team member needs to know or have access to should be included at the top of the process for easy reference. This way, it doesn't clog up the Execution section with too much data.

VIDEO OVERVIEW

This isn't mandatory but can be incredibly helpful. I do most of my work on a computer – this allows me to take screen recordings/screenshots of what I'm doing and saying. I use software called "Loom" for video and good old-fashioned Shift+Command+3 for screenshots. It's awesome and I highly recommend it. If the work you do is out in the field, take videos and photos from your phone to capture the process. They don't have to be production quality. Don't let perfection get in the way of good enough with process documentation. If your work is not easily videoed, I still recommend doing an audio recording of you walking someone through your steps. This is a game-changer for getting new team members up to speed quickly.

APPROVALS

This seems unnecessary when you're small with a handful of people but as you grow, tracking who wrote and approved the process is helpful. This will make innovation of your processes easier and feel less risky when you do have new people onboard. You can see who and when a change was made and easily revert back if it was problematic. Additionally, processes get updated so having a log at the bottom of the sheet for updating changes will ensure that you are up to speed on how recent and up-to-date the information is as well as who owns the changes.

Okay. Now it's your turn. It's time to move from learning to implementing. Pick what you need to most urgently Delegate and create your first SOP. Do not keep reading until you've done this.

I'll still be here.

PROCESS TRACKER

Congratulations! Now that you have your first process, I want to take a step back and give you context on how to create the framework so that this doesn't just become your personal list of processes. That wouldn't be duplicable because the real target is being able to have your processes shared with the organization so that they can learn them and replicate your results. Additionally, you should be expecting that the rest of your leaders are also doing what you are, documenting their processes, so you'll need a centralized place for them to live. In Chapter 17, I'm going to be sharing with you how the heck you incentivize people on your team to document processes because here's the deal: your team hates documentation just as much, if not more, than you do. I have never hired some process fairy who loves nothing more than writing processes all day, every day. It's never happened. So you need to not only become great at this yourself but also align, incentivize, and train your team to document their processes so that they can scale. These org charts demonstrates why this concept is so important:

SMALL ORG CHART

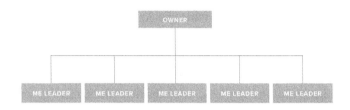

LARGE ORG CHART

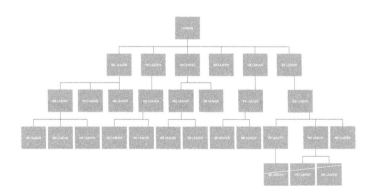

In the first image, it's clear that when you're small, it's easy for you to control processes and be the keeper of all documentation. As you grow – which is why you're reading this book – it's important for you to create processes but the real scale is having your teams create processes and be just as intent on ensuring they're updated, easy to understand, and ever-evolving (more to come on how to do this). For now, I want to share how to set up the Process Tracker.

The first step is to create a Process Tracker document. Maybe you use Excel, or perhaps you're a Google Sheets sort of organization. Regardless of your preferred spreadsheet software, the purpose of this asset is so that you (or the most appropriate member of your team) can document, categorize, and organize all SOPs across your business. Then set up your tracker with the following 4 columns: Column A is the "Department".

Column B is the "Process Name" with a link to the corresponding SOP. Column C is the "Date Approved" and Column D is the "Approver's Initials". That's all. Adding too much information will make this document too difficult to use. Work with your department heads or leaders in your organization to prioritize the processes that are most important to the company's growth. This will help you focus on what will create the most impact.

Entrust your team with this, however, I do recommend that you personally document the processes you're responsible for first so that you can set expectations with the team in terms of how you want this information organized.

*I added the Process Tracker Template to the downloadable at **StartTheWorkTools.com**.*

PROCESS TRACKER

Department	Processes	Date Approved	Approved by
HR	Job Descriptions	06.16.24	ND
HR	Job Posting on Indeed	06.16.23	ND
HR	Job Posting on LinkedIn	11.30.23	ND
HR	Reviewing Resumes	02.06.23	ND
HR	Sourcing Resumes on Indeed	08.11.23	ND
HR	Sourcing Resumes on LinkedIn	01.07.23	ND
HR	Scheduling Interviews	06.17.23	ND
HR	Cultural Interview	08.11.23	ND
HR	Case Study Interview	08.11.24	ND
HR	Core Values Presentation	08.11.25	ND
HR	Offer Letter and Restrictive Covenant Agreement	08.11.21	ND
HR	New Hire Tracker - Pre-First Day	01.06.22	ND
HR	Employee Onboarding Form	01.06.22	ND
HR	Updating the Organizational Chart	06.16.24	ND
HR	Adding Employees to PEO	06.16.23	ND
HR	New Hire Checklist - First Day	11.30.23	ND
HR	Sending Employee Handbook	02.06.23	ND
HR	Sending Incentive Comp Plan	08.11.23	ND
HR	New Hire Orientation	01.07.23	ND
HR	Compliance Training	06.17.23	ND

Remember that Process creates confidence and confidence is the foundation for success. No matter what size your business is — but especially when you're starting out and you have a small team — you need to be documenting what's happening in the organization so that, as you grow, you can duplicate teams and individual roles. For example, let's say you're a single-location business with a plan to grow to six-plus locations in the coming years. You have a front office team member who is responsible for client check-in and check-out both in person and online.

It's a crucial role, one that you're presumably working with this individual to tweak and perfect. Now you might be asking yourself: "Why would I spend my time perfecting the role of the front office? The obvious answer is to ensure your present-day customers experience top-notch service. Which is great... but it's not the only reason. It's imperative to get it right in the first location so that you can duplicate their performance across all future hires since, one day, there will be 6 people simultaneously in this role across different locations. Do you want your clients to all have different experiences at your different locations and share a negative review online about their inconsistent experience? If you're not documenting the best aspects of the current team member's performance, how can you be confident that you'll be able to set up employees two through six for success spread across different locations? You need a foundation to duplicate upon.

TELL ME, SHOW ME, LET ME, COACH ME

For those of you who already have a Process Tracker but struggle to keep it updated, I'd like to introduce you to the Tell Me, Show Me, Let Me, Coach Me framework because this is the mechanism for ensuring that your processes don't collect dust and actually generate a return on investment for you. In my book, *TeamWork*, I introduced and gave the template for creating organizational on-boarding – this is the on-boarding that everyone from your receptionist to your CFO would complete. This is foundational and important data as it's the information that brings every team member up to speed on what your company does, who it services, and points them to the resources that will set them up for success. I have on-boarded thousands of team members, many of them poorly in the early days, so organizational on-boarding needs to be tight.

Training new employees on processes is important because it sets them up for success by ensuring that they have a clear understanding of their responsibilities and how to perform their job effectively. This can improve their efficiency and productivity, reduce the likelihood of mistakes, and increase job satisfaction. A well-designed training program can also help new employees assimilate into the company culture, understand the company's values and goals, and feel valued as a member of the team.

TRAINING TOPIC	TELL ME	SHOW ME	LET ME	COACH ME	COMMENTS & FEEDBACK
Topic that team member will be learning	This column notes the Process to review or who to meet with	This column notes whether you will work with the trainer or watch the recording.	Follow the instructions listed in the box. (INSERT INSTRUCTIONS ON HOW YOU WOULD LIKE TO RECEIVE CONTENT)	Onboarding Mentor is responsible for grading New Team Member using selections below	Onboarding Mentor to leave comments & feedback as applicable
Daily Call Log	Daily Call Log SOP	Calll Log Training Video	Film a zoom with you answering the following questions 1. Tell me when you should be updating this log? 2. What are you responsible for filling out?		
Conducting One-on-One Meetings	We Leadership: One-On-Ones	Shadow your manager leading a One on One with your team member	Invite HR to shadow a One on One with your team member		
Managing Incentive Comp	Managing Incentive Comp (Steps 4-12)	You and your manager will review your team member's incentive comp for the first month of payout together	Complete Incentive Payout for your team, & send to your manager for approval during 2nd month of payout		
Performance Documentation	Using the Department Headcount Tracker	Attend Internal Training with HR to review the process for documenting employee issues	N/A		

Corporate on-boarding is imperative but if you're serious about scaling, the next level of on-boarding should be built out by role. This is where your Process Tracker comes in handy because you're going to use it to create a Tell Me, Show Me, Let Me, Coach Me on-boarding plan for your new hires. But before we build them, it's important to understand why this is needed. This training model is a 4-step process based on adult learning theory that addresses different learning styles and incorporates a variety of teaching methods. By providing a combination of instruction, demonstration, hands-on experience, and feedback, it helps learners to process, retain, and apply information more effectively. By utilizing this model, leaders can create a more effective learning experience that addresses different learning styles and leads to better retention and application of new information and skills. When I say "Leadership is making other people's success easy" this is how you make it easy. You're taking full responsibility for ensuring they understand and have clarity about their role so that they can be successful as quickly as possible. This removes the guessing and uncertainty that can quickly lead to disengagement. Grab the downloadable to follow along with the following explanation of how to create your first Tell Me, Show Me, Let Me, Coach Me on-boarding plan.

The Tell Me phase provides basic instruction and information in a clear and concise manner, which helps learners understand the fundamentals of what they need to know. The Show Me phase demonstrates how the information learned in the Tell Me phase is applied in real-life situations, which helps learners visualize and understand the practical application of the information. The Let Me phase allows learners to apply the information and skills learned in the first two phases by practicing and making mistakes in a controlled environment, which helps to build confidence and reinforce the learning. Finally, the Coach Me phase is the leader's opportunity to give feedback, both positive and negative, so that the team member can improve.

Now let's build an on-boarding plan using this Tell Me, Show Me, Let Me, Coach Me framework. In the first column, you're going to list all of the processes this new hire needs to be trained on. I recommend using the role's job description as the starting point for determining which processes to choose because it will force you to ask "How would this new team member know how to do this?" Ah ha! You should have a process for it! Once you have the process, you list the process, as well as 15-20 others that the team member needs to be trained on to ensure competency. A quick note – you don't have to do the Tell Me, Show Me, Let Me, Coach Me model on every process. This should only be done with the core objectives for the role.

Once you have the process listed (and created) I consider this the Tell component – but make no mistake. The idea isn't that you verbally told them the steps: you told them in writing via an SOP. This is a game changer for ensuring that you've set someone up for success and it removes any internal doubt you may have about whether or not you explained something correctly when you're experiencing performance issues with them later down the line. When you write out your processes, you can be confident that you did your part to set crystal clear expectations. But to take it a step further, you need to move into the Show Me column.

In my world, Show Me oftentimes means that I've recorded a Loom video of me doing each of the steps listed in the process. The majority of the work our teams do is in an office setting and can be recorded. I have, however, rolled this model out with clients who have team members in the field completing a construction job or in a dental office where the work happens in a treatment room. Regardless of where the work is completed, you can't skip the Show Me process as it's a critical component of adult learning. If you're training a hygienist, the Show Me would be the new hire shadowing your current hygienist on their process. If you're training a technician, the team member would go onsite with you and watch how you bend sheet metal at the job site. You get the point. The Show Me component literally means showing the process.

You'll quickly be able to assess your teaching skills and their learning skills through the next step which is Let Me. Now it's their turn to do the work in the same way you did it. There are many ways to do this depending on the work. In our business, we have team members screen record a call of them completing an order and the recording gets linked back to the Tell Me, Show Me, Let Me, Coach Me on-boarding plan for the manager to review. In the hygienist example, the new provider would be completing the cleaning and the leader would be watching and reviewing the work. In the Let Me phase, there should always be feedback immediately afterward. Make feedback normal in your organization. If they did something wrong, call it out and be specific. This leads us to the Coach Me phase.

It's not good enough to just tell someone how to do something and then expect that they can do it. Your clients, customers, or patients need to experience similar quality across all people they interact with in your business. This is how a business's reputation either flourishes or plummets. I can't tell you how many times I've fallen in love with a restaurant and found out that they have another location in a city I'm visiting. I'm met with disappointment when I find that location to be nothing like the original. It degrades the brand when this happens and is a letdown to your customers. This is why, after you've done all of the setup for telling, showing, and letting a new team member be an extension of your brand, you must be willing to coach them early and often. In this column, I link out a feedback form so the team member knows and expects that they will be receiving feedback. It doesn't have to be complicated. The feedback I give focuses first on asking what they think went well and what they could have improved. This helps me understand if they're aware of their strengths and areas of opportunities. If we're in alignment, great! Then I share that with them. If not, I use this as a coaching opportunity to point out additional areas that could have gone differently and role-play additional scenarios to ensure they are fully competent.

At this point, you get to determine if their performance is in alignment with your standards. If it's not, they should not be responsible for that process until they've created confidence in you that they're ready. This is my personal policy. If I don't feel confident, I'm not Delegating it and it stays as my Continue. This policy allows me to sleep like a baby, even with hundreds of employees. When you have confidence that things are being done correctly because you've coached your team members, you will have restful nights too.

WHERE TO START?

Creating training like this is not fun. I will be the first to admit that. When you start this, you just have to rip the band-aid off and get going – one role at a time. I would suggest that you start in one of two places: if you have an existing team member who is causing trouble in the business but you don't feel comfortable firing them because it would leave a gaping hole, start the process documentation with that role. If you aren't experiencing this currently, look at your 1-year revenue targets (if you don't know how to set these, go to Chapter 12) and identify which roles you will need to duplicate in order to hit the target. These are normally revenue-generating roles or fulfillment roles. Start there.

At this point, you should be convinced that even though this work may not be fun, it certainly is sexy once you put it all together. Because you've done the work that sets your team up for massive success, which by default does the same for you and your business. This means you've done something most business owners only dream about: you've given yourself the most valuable resource there is – time. Time is at an absolute premium for business owners; you know that. So now you've got a reliable roadmap, the blueprint, and the undeniable structure to control your time and your business through the power of processes. It's time to Start The Work.

*All the exclusive resources I mention in the book are ready for you to use, along with videos, tools, and extras that I couldn't share in this book, go to **StartTheWorkTools.com**.*

YOU

- ☑ SACRIFICES
- ☑ LET'S MAKE PROCESSES SEXY
- ☑ **MORNING ROUTINE**
- ☐ INBOX ZERO

CHAPTER 8

MORNING ROUTINE

All hail for the unveiling of the world's greatest morning routine that will get you the results you're looking for: Start the work. No seriously – as quickly as you can get out of bed and make yourself coffee, then start the work. This is what I do 365 days per year. It's not sexy and it doesn't put you in the perfect state for you to feel bliss and grateful that Mother Earth gave you the gift of life today. That's fine for someone else but take a moment and read what the title of this chapter is: *Morning Routine for People Who Want to Achieve Their Goals.*

Many people are keen on figuring out the most ideal morning routine because it is often seen as a life hack. You believe that by having a specific routine in the morning, you'll be at an optimal state to magically achieve your laundry list of to-dos by following a made-up list of tasks to start your day. Hear me loud and clear: There is no hack! Stop listening to the motivational speakers, productivity experts, and influencers on social media who share their morning routine as a glamorized "process" – with the holy-grail for why they're a bazillionaire. Let's not confuse causation and correlation.

So let's break down why having the perfect morning routine is a crock of shit, shall we? Everyone is different, what works for one person may not work for another. Ask 5 billionaires what their morning routines are and you will get 5 different answers. Jeff Bezos wakes up at 6:30, makes breakfast and coffee, and states that his "puttering around time is important" to him in the morning so he doesn't get to the office until around 10 am. Elon Musk, on the other hand, wakes up at 7, skips breakfast, but shares that he always finds time for a shower as it's the source of his great ideas. Mark Zuckerberg is up around 8 and instantly starts scrolling through Meta, Messenger, and WhatsApp. There is no secret step that's universally followed by all successful people. A morning routine is not a necessity for success; it's just one of many tools that may help someone achieve their goals. Success is not dependent on one factor. There are many nuances including hard work, perseverance, and talent – not just a morning routine.

Another inherent issue with creating this mandatory list of things you have to do to "set your day up for success" is this: what happens when you can't complete a step? Are you now unable to have a productive day because you're reliant on your routine to make your day go right? "You" make your day go right. Not the 15-minute walk, meditation, gratitude practice, grounding, and green juice you drink. When you give credit to and create dependencies on the perfect set of circumstances, you are giving away your power.

The reality is you didn't pick up this book to find yourself or explore the meaning of life. You desire to turn into the leader your business needs. That is the phase of life you're in. I am certain that you will have other phases where different interests in your life will be a priority and your business won't be your focus. But in this phase, you and I are operating on the same wavelength and the question you find yourself asking is "How can I reach my potential?"

My strong recommendation for you is to start the most important work as quickly as possible. My mornings do start early but not because I'm trying to game some system. I go to bed at 9:30pm and wake up around 5:15am. I get to my Keurig machine within 90 seconds of waking up; make my coffee, so that I'm sitting at my desk no later than 5:30am. From there, I work on the things that are the most pressing. A tip that's always helped me is planning the next day before leaving work. I spend 3-5 minutes reviewing my calendar, projects, and emails so that I have my "Top Priorities list" for the next morning. That way, when my eyes are still heavy at 5:00am, I don't have to think about all of the things I could do – I just start on the list I've already made and work my way through it. I do find that mornings and evenings are the best times for me to get my actual work done as most days I'm in meetings, creating content, or talking with people to move initiatives forward. The evenings I reserve for emails as I try not to waste the mornings when I can do deeper work than responding to emails. My mornings are largely spent on the projects from my "Start" list to ensure that they're accomplished. I'm a big believer in the saying "First things first". If you know you need to get it done, do it first.

The idea of the perfect morning routine is a myth. Everyone is different and what works for one person may not work for another. Instead of focusing on creating the perfect morning routine, focus on starting the most important work as quickly as possible. Planning the next day before leaving work and taking advantage of the best times of the day for you to work, such as mornings and evenings, can help set you up for success. Remember, you are in control of your day and your success, not a set of tasks or a specific routine.

I give you permission to start the work right away in the morning. Rather than absorbing the routines of anyone else who, frankly, isn't you and isn't responsible for your results. Of course you don't have to mirror my method; this is just what works for me. I never regret starting the work first thing, but always regret putting off what needs to get done, as it feels like a setback when the momentum of the day gets underway.

All the exclusive resources I mention in the book are ready for you to use, along with videos, tools, and extras that I couldn't share in this book, go to StartTheWorkTools.com.

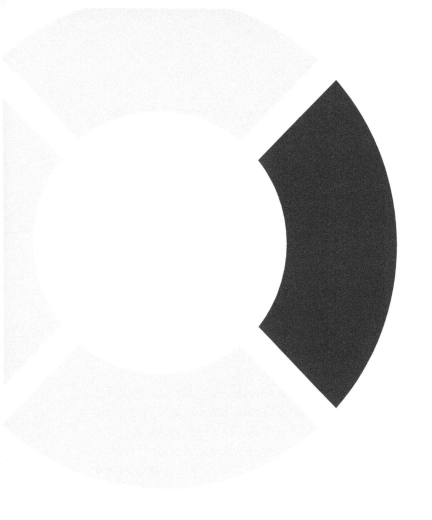

YOU

- ☑ SACRIFICES
- ☑ LET'S MAKE PROCESSES SEXY
- ☑ MORNING ROUTINE
- ☑ **INBOX ZERO**

66/99

CHAPTER 9

INBOX ZERO

This is often times the most unpopular conversation I have with leaders but I can't write a book about how to grow a business without acknowledging one of the least effective yet ever-present time sucks: emails. I find there are 2 types of emailers: you inconsistently pick and choose what you'll read and respond to or you spend an ungodly amount of time answering them and then feeling anxious when you get behind and they start piling up.

Emails have become an integral part of running a business. They allow you a chance to connect with clients, partners, and employees, and build relationships that can take your business to new heights. They can also be a source of stress, anxiety, and distraction. The constant influx of messages can leave you feeling overwhelmed and disconnected from what truly matters.

Managing your own inbox allows for direct, immediate communication with clients and partners. It's an opportunity to build trust, address concerns, and resolve issues in real-time, which can be invaluable in a fast-paced growth environment. It also allows for better organization, control, and efficiency in terms of communication and productivity.

Imagine the world before emails. You had to either be in a meeting with someone or call them in order to communicate an idea, update, proposal, or issue. Emails are an effective use of time because they allow for quick and efficient communication. They can be sent and received instantly, which allows for a faster exchange of information than traditional meetings or phone calls. They can be easily organized and stored, making it easy to access and reference important information and allow for easy communication with multiple people at once, which can save a lot of time compared to having individual conversations. Emails also allow for asynchronous communication, meaning that the sender and receiver don't need to be online at the same time. This allows for a more flexible communication style, where people can respond at their convenience, which can be especially useful for people working in different time zones or for those who have busy schedules.

On the other hand, let's not sugarcoat it; dealing with an overwhelming amount of emails can be a real pain in the ass. It's hard to separate the wheat from the chaff and it's easy to get bogged down by the constant influx of messages. It can lead to missed opportunities and important information being overlooked. Your inbox can leave you feeling the need to constantly check your email and wondering when the flood of new messages will stop.

On top of that, have you ever thought about how un-scalable your time sending emails is?

When you look at your Duplication Activity – did you include how much time you're spending on emails? If it's more than 30 minutes per day, let's figure out how to decrease this activity. If you are spending hours every day responding to emails, you can't possibly be spending the time you need to on sales, marketing, and business development. Do not forget your role! Generating revenue is the core purpose of any business, and it's crucial for the survival and success of a business. If you are not focused on revenue growth, you're foolishly prioritizing being a manager instead of an entrepreneur.

This is why it's essential to get your priorities aligned with your business target. If you have a $5m business and a target of making it a $50m business, I can assure you that you will not find the $45m sitting inside your inbox. So how do you navigate your time spent on email?

Since emails are a part of today's business communication landscape, let's dive into how to create an email culture in your business that helps you stay focused on revenue while not being out of the loop on important initiatives.

On the note of Email Culture, I will say that the way the leader handles emails is how the environment handles emails. If you are up all hours of the night and weekends sending long emails with bulleted lists, I can assure you that your team will believe that it is an expectation. Equally, if you never respond to emails, you can inadvertently create a non-responsive dynamic in your team which doesn't suit your customers or important internal communication. Culture starts at the top so let's unpack how you can intentionally create your company's email culture.

EMAIL RULES

Rule #1: Spend less than 30 minutes per day in your inbox. This is your guiding light and should be your target if you're a chronic emailer. I used to really struggle to find the balance between responding to emails and doing actual work as it started to feel like answering my emails was my job. I would spend 3 hours a day responding to a never-ending list of emails just to let 2 hours pass and find my inbox back up to hundreds. If you are in the same position, this 30-minute rule will be a game changer. If you told yourself that you only have 30 minutes to dedicate to your inbox, what emails wouldn't you read? What information do you actually not need? Who should be taking more responsibility in your organization for the items you can't get to? What lists can you be removed from? Which projects actually need your attention? When you start to ask yourself these questions, you will create solutions. This is the magic of being a leader and owning your time. No one is forcing you to do this – it's a choice. Don't choose a life shackled to your inbox; 30 minutes each day should give you enough time.

I'm also a stickler about ripping the band-aid off. Rapid change forces change. If you're currently spending hours each day, don't try to wean yourself down incrementally. This is a new policy for you starting today. Ready, set, reprioritize.

Now that you have extra time back, consult your Duplication Activity. What do you need to get done that will push your business forward? Go do that in replacement. Remember: I'm not encouraging you to stop working so that you can eat bonbons and binge your favorite TV show. The target is to free your time up to allow yourself the space to duplicate you inside your business.

Rule #2: Always address who you are talking to. This sounds like a no-brainer but it's a hard learned lesson. When you don't address who you are looking for a response from, you reduce your chances of getting a response. It's easy to think your team is the problem and they're so slow to get back to you, however, I have a sinking suspicion that you do not make it easy on them to know exactly what you want and from whom. Even if the email is to multiple people, put specific initials by the items you want the individuals to address. An inordinate amount of time is wasted in email communication simply because the recipient is unclear that you're looking for a specific response.

Rule #3: Determine when you need a response. Ahhh – Rule #2 and #3 go hand in hand. Set a timeline. If you need a response by EOD, tomorrow at noon, or the first Tuesday of next month, say that. Put yourself in your team's shoes. If they don't know when you want something, they're likely treating everything you ask for like a fire. They're dropping the responsibilities of their current role to pick up whatever it is you just asked for – which maybe that's what you intended! But many times, it's not and you know that you could have waited. Interestingly enough, this is what often creates undue inefficiencies inside your team to where they feel "burnt out" or "overwhelmed". It is likely that they actually have enough time in a 40-hour work week, if used efficiently, to complete the work for their role. What's actually happening when they're requesting more resources or feeling overwhelmed is they don't know how to prioritize the work so your deadline and the deadlines of their existing projects all come at the same time. If you can, avoid this as much as possible by giving clear deadlines.

Money loves speed and I'm a big proponent of moving quickly. Having grown from 0 to 220+ team members in 4 years, my team and our results can confirm that I move quickly. However, it's critical to move quickly and efficiently as you scale. The efficiency comes in through setting clear timelines and expectations with my team. You can push hard while giving visibility to what your team's work will look like in the coming weeks. Creating an environment where "everything needs to get done now" is problematic to long-term engagement with your team members. Make deadlines clear and real in your emails. No one likes to be rushed for no reason –

especially when they're making sacrifices to pull something off.

Rule #4: Pick up the phone. If the back and forth about a decision goes on for more than 3 emails, pick up the freakin' phone. Don't waste your time and the time of others going on and on in an email chain. Unless the situation needs to be documented for legal reasons, just pick up the phone and talk through the situation.

Rule #5: Celebrate in public, correct in private. This is a rule that applies to all communication, but especially email. As the leader, it's important to celebrate team wins and acknowledge when a target was hit. If a team lead announces their team hit a target on their end-of-week report, I'm all for you hitting "reply all" and giving a thumbs up and a nice acknowledgment. You'll notice that I said their team "hit a target" – this is worthy of acknowledgment and celebration. You should not set the tone that you give kudos when nothing substantial has happened – there shouldn't be participation awards in your business communication because the rest of your team is constantly observing what you do and don't acknowledge. The bar should be set high.

On the flip side, when a situation arises via email that needs to be corrected, this should happen only with the team member it involves. There's no need to bring other team members into issues that should be handled in private. Correcting people in your company is your job. The reality is you did not hire robots who will execute flawlessly on every initiative and read your mind to know how to handle all situations exactly like you would want. Normalize giving corrective feedback via email immediately. It doesn't need to wait for an in-person conversation – it can be handled instantly with a short, non-emotional response. The way to normalize this is to only direct your feedback to one person as it becomes a coaching opportunity. When you do it in front of others, it can lead to defensiveness since they likely want to save face with their peers. Even if the defensiveness isn't overt in their response back, you've created a distraction with them and the others on the communication line that's no longer focused on the business. This is not ideal so keep it between you and the person you're correcting.

When you get clear and intentional about how you use your inbox and email communication, you will see a result that leads to more effective communication across your company and team. It can take new team members awhile to figure out the email culture in your business and I'm not one to leave these types of things to chance so I've created Email Best Practices that all new hires receive to set expectations. If you'd like to shamelessly steal it, here it is:

EMAIL BEST PRACTICES

VISION:

These are best practices that we expect all team members to adhere when communicating with co-workers and clients. The manner in which you utilize email communication is a direct reflection of our brand and you as a professional.

Below are recommendations on how to use email more effectively to communicate to your audience in the most professional and efficient manner.

TIPS:

1. REREAD EVERY EMAIL TWICE BEFORE SENDING.
2. Always address who you are talking to - do not send "Hey Team," emails if you're looking for a response from a specific person. When addressing a group, you should open with "Hey Team," but then put the name(s) of the people you need specific responses from.
3. When you are looking for a response, request a specific date that you need a response by.
4. Be known as someone others can depend on for a response.
5. Clean out your inbox weekly.
6. Respond as quickly as possible on internal emails - don't take longer than 48 hours.
7. If you are collecting data to respond, confirm that you received the email and let the recipient know when they can expect a response back.
8. Avoid using negative words like "unfortunately". It sets the person up for a negative statement and makes the situation seem worse than it actually is.
   - Focus on what you can do
   - Always agree - acknowledge, duplicate, transition
   - "Absolutely! Of course! No Problem! Would love to! Love it!"
9. Overdeliver on responses. Provide extra value and value-added follow up.
10. Avoid the "back and forth" as much as possible.
    - Use the "3-email guideline" - If you have to go back and forth on an email more than 3 times, pick up the phone.
    - Sometimes it's better and more effective to just call!
11. Be quick...speed to service. A client should not have to wait more than a few hours for a response. An email/text/missed call should be responded to within 24 hours.
12. If you aren't sure how to respond or if you need to respond, ask! It's better to communicate than stay silent.
13. Think revenue: Flip service calls/emails to revenue. A lot of the deals that are closed originate from requests or cancellations.
14. Use our standard fonts, grammar, formatting and sentence structure.
15. Consider the use of bullets to summarize points and make it easier for the recipient to understand intentions.
16. Do not use email if you expect an immediate response. Consider Slack messages, text or call.
17. Set automated out of office notifications when you will be away for more than 24 hrs. The notification should include your return date and who should be contacted if an immediate response is required.

Since I'm dishing out tips, I'd be remiss if I didn't tell you about an email lifesaver. About a year and a half ago, I started using a tool called "Superhuman" to gamify my inbox. This tool has been a game changer for me as it has functions to remind me of important messages, auto follow up with certain email addresses, and organize and search messages. By using Superhuman, I am not only able to clear out my inbox quickly, but I am also able to keep track of my progress and see how many weeks in a row I have been able to hit inbox zero. This makes the process more enjoyable and less of a chore. Sometimes it's the incremental tweaks that make all the difference.

By now, you should notice a pattern here. You're building structure in your day to leverage and maximize your time in a way that produces meaningful results. A structure that, although it may be difficult at first, allows you to continue growing and building and expanding rather than keeping you stuck spinning your wheels. I see this far too often with clients who struggle to adapt their schedule and their approach so they end up stalling. By default, this unwillingness to build and follow a structure for their own time, limits their ability to duplicate themselves in their business. Remember, your business can only grow to the level you're willing to grow.

Your business is a mirror, reflecting exactly how you're showing up. So if you don't establish boundaries, dial in your ability to get to work on the most important things first, and start setting rules around your primary communication tool and time potential thief – email, then your company culture will show the same thing (which I'll go into detail within the next section). Yet, if you want your business to mirror back what you say you want, then you need to lead by example, set the standard, and you'll quickly see your business start to follow your lead.

With the structure you're putting in place, you're stacking the building blocks necessary to grow, scale, and duplicate your efforts. Which, as a result, is how your business will do the same and you'll start to scale faster than you can imagine. This concept is important, so to drive it home, realize this ability to create structure around your time is the core difference between Sarah Scales and Sean Stagnates; one has mastered their time, while the other is a slave to it. This shows up in daily life personally and professionally.

YOUR
CULTURE

- → MISSION/VISION/CORE VALUES
- → PROMOTION
- → ANNUAL PLANNING
- → QUARTERLY TEAM MEETINGS
- → A HEALTHY MEETING CULTURE

YOUR CULTURE

We've been focused on applying Stop, Continue, Delegate, and Start to you, now it's time to consider how your time impacts your culture and how you can set up processes (there's that sexy word again) to make your operations run like clockwork, with or without you.

This may sound like a pipedream at this point, or maybe you've had some success with duplication and growth but are having a hard time troubleshooting your current bottleneck. This can be a very frustrating place to be. You're not alone. I've been there before, as have many other successful business owners I've worked with. We want to facilitate a massive breakthrough in your culture. This is arguably the most important place you can spend your time because it creates the foundation of your business.

Each of the following chapters will build on each other to help you see the power of the results you create when you start the work of solidifying your company culture. This is where you declare what you stand for, who you're helping, and align people in your purpose as a company. It's also some of my most favorite topics to coach business owners on because I know how powerful it is when they take the culture seriously. If you don't intentionally start the work to shape your culture – it will be formed without you. Culture is organic, like a garden. You can tend to it, pluck weeds, and nurture it into a direction that's best for everyone – or it can be left to grow wild and messy.

When scaling, it's important to remember that you can either control your culture or your culture can control you. We see this in the way many business owners are approaching the conversation around remote versus in-person work. No matter where you stand on the topic, are you being direct with your team and making a decision around it, or are you waffling back and forth and unwilling to draw a line in the sand? If you are, you're leaving your company's culture to figure itself out. This scales nothing but chaos.

It's time to get clear on your Mission, Vision, and Values. It's time to start promoting to the world what your business is all about. It's time to start tactically acting out those Core Values and principles through annual and quarterly team meetings that reinforce a culture of excellence from the top to the bottom of your organization.

Let's start the work on your culture.

All the exclusive resources I mention in the book are ready for you to use, along with videos, tools, and extras that I couldn't share in this book, go to StartTheWorkTools.com.

YOUR CULTURE

- ☑ **MISSION/VISION/CORE VALUES**
- ☐ PROMOTION
- ☐ ANNUAL PLANNING
- ☐ QUARTERLY TEAM MEETINGS
- ☐ A HEALTHY MEETING CULTURE

CHAPTER 10

MISSION, VISION, VALUES

As I'm writing, I can look down and see a sticky note that I permanently leave on my desk that says: "R = P today?" This shorthand stands for: Does my Reality equal my Potential today? I keep this in front of me as a constant reminder of why I'm doing what I'm doing. Day to day, in between meetings, emails, unanswered text messages, and a list of things that need to get done, I can often find myself getting frustrated and overwhelmed. If I'm honest, I don't enjoy doing most of what I do. It's a never-ending cycle of squeezing in as much as possible in order to move my priorities forward. I rarely feel up to all of the responsibility. This isn't meant to be my "Woe is me" moment – I just want to be honest about what the work really feels like. I called this book Start the Work because reaching your potential is going to require work. Lots of it. I'm not here to sugar-coat that.

If you're anything like me, you are likely disappointed when you think about your potential because your reality isn't in line with your potential. You see a version of yourself who has accomplished more and contributed more than you currently have to show. Looking at the amount of people you've impacted can be discouraging. If we've impacted 250,000 business owners in the last five years – that's the reality. But is our potential higher? What if we had the potential to serve 5 million business owners? If that's the case, my Reality most definitely isn't equaling my Potential – and we have our work cut out for us to fix it. Our reality is always shifting. So is our understanding of what we have the potential for. When you're clear on your why, you must translate it into a Mission statement for your team. As with any great Mission, when you've presented it properly and reinforced it in the way that you hire and develop your team – it should ignite your team and provide clarity in times of uncertainty. On an emotional level, the Mission statement will be a rallying cry that you will use to warm people up to the change that growth brings – scaling takes everybody out of their comfort zone. For people to be willing to be taken out of their comfort zone, they have to know why.

On the practical side of things, the Mission keeps everyone, including you, on the same page. Things get chaotic. It's so easy to lose the plot in the shuffle of change. A clear Mission keeps everyone grounded, even while things soar. Just like you needed a "why" to spark the initial creation of your business, you need a "why" to scale. Let's take a step back and put your Mission statement under the microscope: is it big enough to motivate your growth? If you haven't done so already, grab the downloadable at *StartTheWorkTools.com* in order to get complete access to the Mission/Vision/Values

Activity. This will be a helpful guide throughout this chapter.

WHEN SCALING SERVES THE MISSION

Being clear on your Mission will serve you greatly as you parse out the best places to put your time. Knowing exactly why your business exists naturally informs how best to analyze your schedule and categorize what needs to be Stopped, Started, Delegated, and Continued. And remember, it's not just about you, this is also about your team (we're not here to micromanage, which is the opposite of scaling). The Mission serves as a filter for their new ideas and opportunities to be run through. This is how you scale through people. Don't just make the effort to set a Mission, take the time to review and share it daily. This will keep you focused and open to the things on your calendar that actually matter in the big picture.

Your current Mission is either conducive to growth, or it isn't. Your business could be a seed, a flower, or a tree. In any case, a plant can only grow as big as the pot that it's put in. Your Mission statement is that pot – the aspiration you are scaling to chase. Your mission statement has to be big.

At Cardone Ventures, our Mission is to help business owners achieve their personal, professional, and financial goals, through the growth of their businesses. The scope remains large – we can be certain that there will never be a shortage of business owners we can build relationships with and help them thrive in their industries. We could scale our business internationally – and our Mission would never be totally satisfied to the point where we could pat ourselves on the back and retire to complacency.

Expanding your offerings, growing your team, and increasing the amount of revenue flowing into your business is a desirable outcome, yes, but the process of getting there can be painful for both you and your team. From their perspective, they have to deal with change. Systems are being updated, procedures are changing, and new skills need to be acquired to proactively tackle issues that you know are coming down the line. Because they don't see the future from your vantage point – your team may not understand why these changes are necessary. It may feel to them as though you're shaking things up simply for the sake of shaking things up – adding more and more with no rhyme or reason. Obviously, transparency is hugely important, but even when the reason for change is clear, change can still be unsettling.

A bold mission statement – one that rings true to all levels of your organization – will help you get your culture to understand why you're pushing so hard: in the name of the goals that are bigger and more attractive than the prospects of things just staying the same. In my book *TeamWork*, I dive into exactly how to draft and roll out your Mission, Vision, and Values statements. If you want the step by step guide, get your copy at *CardoneVentures.com/Teamwork*.

OVERCOMING COMPLACENCY

Complacency is likely the reason that your business hasn't been scaling, so here's some tough love. First, if you are becoming complacent, you aren't spending enough time around people that are expanding your perspective of what's possible. Ask yourself these questions: When was the last time I gave $1m to charity? How is my community better off because of the abundant success I'm having? When was the last time someone told me "thank you" for changing their life? If you don't feel good about your answers to these questions, you've still got a lot of work to do.

Second, being complacent is selfish. Seriously. When I'm working with a client who is struggling to establish quantifiable goals, or unwilling to update and expand their goals, I often ask them why they are being so selfish. If Sarah Scales really believes that she delivers the best dental work in the city of Phoenix, Arizona, couldn't that city hold 15 of her locations? How many dental practices are there in Phoenix and how many patients are you allowing to go to competitors that don't take their care to heart like you do? If Sarah Scales thinks that she's "good" at $5 million dollars and starts coasting, she's closing the door on more people that want to be helped.

The lesson is this: if you really believe in the product or service that you offer, you are doing people a disservice by not going full steam ahead to scale.

SHINY OBJECTS SYNDROME

The Mission also helps you maintain clarity as you grow. Entrepreneurs are big dreamers – so we can sometimes get distracted. Sarah Scale's Mission statement is "We help people feel confident in their smile". If she had an opportunity to expand and add a yoga studio to her practice, there's no confusion about what the right decision is. I'm sure she is passionate about downward dogs and high lunges, but this is not going to take her in the direction of her overarching Mission. Instead, the resources for that addition would be better spent in adding a CEREC machine that will allow for same-day crowns or incorporating orthodontic services to offer everything people need for a confident smile.

This is not to say that diversifying your business is a bad thing – it just needs to be run through the filter of your Mission. Otherwise, every family venture or Tom, Dick, and Harry who approaches you with an exciting new opportunity will distract you from your why. If you are going to expand beyond the previously stated boundaries of your Mission, ask yourself this: is this connected or disconnected to my business? Anything disconnected should be avoided until you have a liquidity event or exit.

A VISION TO SCALE

After the Mission comes the Vision. Vision is a matter of deciding and proclaiming where you are going. There was a time before smartphones and GPS, when people had to trace their road trip plans on paper maps with highlighters. There is no GPS for scaling a business. Designing a business is much like tracing out a route on a map by hand, weighing the decision of every turn, comparing different paths forward, and trying your damnedest to anticipate where the traffic jams will be.

The Vision is long-term. It has to shift every so often as you advance along the road. The Vision is the most important foundation for the constant reassessment of where you, your leaders, and your team members are spending their time. With a clear direction, you can frame the question of "where should I be spending my time" based on the stated place you are going. If you aren't spending any of your time, reference your Duplication Activity, on where you've said you're going, it shouldn't be a surprise to you that you aren't getting close. Devoid of the Vision, it's easy to think that you're making progress when in reality, you're just busy. Don't confuse the two.

Working together, your Mission and Vision inform your decision making. If you spend time dwelling on them, they will become ingrained and make you really clear on where your time and energy need to go. Before we were working on hard and fast categorizations about where you're spending time. Now, we're building your understanding of the Mission and Vision that will allow you to gut-check the usefulness of everything to your ultimate goals. The Vision is just as much for you as it is for your team. Once you get yourself clear on how to align your time with your Vision, you need to train your team to do the same. Only when you and your leaders are focused on this, does scaling become part of your culture.

While the Mission is broad, expansive, and intentionally left open-ended, your Vision has to be quantifiable. It highlights what it's going to look like to scale your business – so make it trackable and be sure that there are numbers attached to it. Knowing where you want your company to head is the only way you'll have certainty that your time is going to good use.

Your Visions represents your 10-year milestone.

10 years from today...

- What is my business worth?
- How many people do I employ?
- How many clients or customers has my business impacted?

Think about it like this: if you spent 10 years earnestly and diligently chasing the Mission that you've laid out, what would the result be?

But as we've discussed earlier, that Vision can and should shift. Our Vision is to help 1 million business owners 10X. In years 1 to 5, I'm counting how many people we are actually helping. So, if in year 5 we'd only impacted

500,000 people (half our target in half the time), we wouldn't be in a position to change it.

But if we have impacted 800,000 people in those 5 years, we have to update and expand the Vision – otherwise, we run the risk of undershooting our potential.

STICKING TO YOUR VALUES

The glue that defines and brings cohesion to your culture are your Core Values. As you scale, staying true to your principles as a business leader will become more difficult by the day. More people will inevitably be involved with your day-to-day operations. The decisions you make will come with bigger implications. The amount of unclear situations you find yourself in will multiply. Without Core Values your team can stick to, you'll be constantly trying to reinforce principles inside your culture when you never told anybody they exist.

Let's go back to the late nineties. TLC's "No Scrubs" is topping the charts. A company called Google is trying to monetize its search engine. This represented the first round of scaling for a business that would, in a couple decades, be worth $1,135 billion – and hold over 90% market share in their industry. When changes come, it's easy to lose sight of your core values. Ahead of a key PR meeting with the Washington Post – a Google engineer went into the board room and wrote "Don't Be Evil" on the whiteboard.

This would become – for a time – a motto of Google's. I'm not here to question whether they continue to live up to this standard, but the story highlights the importance of going into scaling only after you are crystal clear on what your values are. As you grow, more people get involved and the implications of your decisions get bigger. You can start with a loose idea of not wanting to be evil – but what does that look like once you've hit the trials that are to come? Your values can't just be platitudes that sound right, noble, or good to you. They have to represent principles that you're not going to fail to live up to. Your values should reflect who you are in good times and bad. They are the core principles you lean on when making difficult decisions with your time: investments, hiring, partnerships, evaluating vendors – the list goes on.

SCALING WITH INTEGRITY

Just as you need to continue to live up to your outlined Values, the team members you hire as you scale will need to equally subscribe to them. Remaining consistent with them and leading by example will help you during any difficult conversation or crossroads to come. Let's say somebody's not meeting their performance standards – or worse, there's an ethical gap that needs to be addressed. If you haven't laid out your Values, then having a meaningful conversation with this team member becomes all the more difficult. The standards haven't been laid out, nor reinforced, so you're going to come off as the asshole boss simply out to get them.

So if you say your business values discipline – but you don't have discipline – you're setting yourself up for failure. You're putting something out into the environment that doesn't exist. Its lack will only become more exposed and apparent the larger you scale. Imagine being a fitness trainer and telling your clients that they should be waking up at 5 am to work out, but you're sleeping in till 7 am every morning, boozing it up the night before, and stumbling into the gym as a total hot mess. You're violating your ability to trust yourself and it's even harder to truly help your clients get their desired results because you don't practice what you preach.

But if you have created intentions around Core Values and you continue to live them out – even in the chaos of scaling – you have a framework for the person falling short to understand where they're off and how the problem can be fixed. This is how culture is truly defined.

INTENTIONALLY WITH YOUR CULTURE

Your business is only going to get more complicated and complex as it scales. When push comes to shove – the quality of your Mission, Vision, and Core Values should remain as the filters for your decisions and where you spend your time. These are the aspirations of your company, in both the long and short term. Just like driving a car, you're going to go in the direction that has your attention. Once you've created a Mission, Vision, and Core Values that are optimized for growth, don't just put them in a handbook and file them away. These make up the foundation that will prioritize your and your team's time in the future and the coordinates that will determine where you go as you scale. When you're small, these cultural necessities seem to be unnecessary. But that's only the perspective of Sean Stagnates who doesn't realize the direction he needs to set for the hundreds of people he'll hire in the future. Sally, on the other hand, has laid the groundwork today because she's clear on what she's doing: scaling.

And because scaling is the goal, understanding what it is you're trying to scale, why, and creating the right filter to make decisions that move your business forward is crucial. Without the building blocks of a compelling Mission, a Vision worth fighting for, and a set of Core Values representing the essence of who you are, and what you stand for, scaling becomes more of an illusion than a reality.

All the exclusive resources I mention in the book are ready for you to use, along with videos, tools, and extras that I couldn't share in this book, go to StartTheWorkTools.com.

YOUR
CULTURE

- ☑ MISSION/VISION/CORE VALUES
- ☑ **PROMOTION**
- ☐ ANNUAL PLANNING
- ☐ QUARTERLY TEAM MEETINGS
- ☐ A HEALTHY MEETING CULTURE

CHAPTER 11

PROMOTION

"You're robbing the world of your talents if you're not willing to get over your fear of being seen". Those are the words of my friend Pete Vargas. Before Brandon and I were partnered with the Cardones, we had attended one of their events and Pete was an incredible speaker who shared that line in a way that really resonated with me.

Throughout my twenties, I was plagued with horrible stage fright. I wouldn't speak in a meeting that had more than three or so people in it – much less in front of an audience. Here was Pete, saying this fear was causing me to rob the world of something it needed. Hearing him speak in 2019 put me on a path that would see me speaking on stage, teaching large courses, and writing two books (as of the one that's currently in your hands). I had to attack my fear of having people look at me which was deeply rooted in not believing I was good enough and worrying that people wouldn't think I'm some dumb blonde gold digger. In order to overcome this fear, my first step was launching my podcast. Starting out, it was more exposure therapy than anything. It was horrifying – the idea of my voice just being out on the internet forever.

Listening back to early episodes now makes me cringe. But as with anything, you get a certain amount of reps in and you get better.

In 4 years, I've generated over $10m from YouTube and podcasts alone.

What's cool is that my stage fright is no longer my story. My prep time used to be consumed with trying to calm down my nerves. Now, I'm using that time to consider what the audience needs, taking feedback, and shaping my communication in a way that serves a valuable purpose. It's not about what Natalie needs. It's about what the audience needs. My fear of what other people think doesn't have a place in that equation. Maybe you resonate with this – and know what it's like to have a fear of attention, public speaking, or what other people are going to think. Whether you like it or not, if you are going to scale your organization, we are going to have to get you over this fear.

Let's unpack why.

YOUR PRIMARY FUNCTION

What's your job as the leader of a scaling business? A lot of things probably come to mind. At Cardone Ventures, clients are sometimes surprised when we tell them that a business owner's primary function in the organization is to get known. You need to get yourself, your business, and your product/service known at all costs. The reality is you can have the best product, an amazing service, and the most fantastic retention program – but if no one knows you exist, none of that matters.

Most business owners get caught up in making their products and services perfect. Before launching, they spend thousands of hours to craft the perfect offering and planning the execution from A-Z. The challenge is, they've wasted all of this time building something when they don't even know if demand exists! Instead of spending this time pouring themselves into the "perfect" product, they should be promoting the product. Why does Tesla rollout their new models and take deposits years before they are in production? Elon is a master promoter. He's funding the build and getting customer insights at the same time. If no one put a deposit down, do you think he'd still build the car? Of course not. There's no demand.

Additionally, once you have pre-sold your new idea, you have renewed excitement about completing the work. With customers waiting, you'll be laser focused on delivering what you promised instead of tinkering and procrastinating to get the product launched. This is a little hack I learned from Grant Cardone – whenever you're procrastinating, start promoting. If you've always wanted to run a marathon but keep putting it off year after year, get on social media and proclaim to the world that you're running a marathon by the end of this year. Guess what's going to happen next? You'll sign up for that marathon. Why? You've just promoted that you would! Promotion is the ultimate procrastination hack.

Now I know that it's "cool" to go into hiding to put work in on yourself and come out months later as a new you. I've often heard the quote "Don't tell people what you're going to do. Just do it and shock them". So dumb! You increase your likelihood of doing it when you have accountability because people are driven by not wanting to look like you failed. So decrease your chances of failing and start promoting what you're procrastinating.

If you want to be the leader of a scaling business? Guess what – your place will be on the growth side of the business. If you want to bolster your organization's brand the responsibility falls on you. As the creator, founder, and owner of this thing, it's your job to make it known. You are the source of your organization's promotion – you cannot abdicate this. Agencies can help, yes. But if you aren't taking the lead, they aren't going to magically create a brand better than you are for your business. This is the fallacy of hiring an agency. They will never care more than you about your brand and success. You can take the lazy route and think that because they are the "experts" that they should be responsible. Just acknowledge that you're abdicating your role.

So what does promotion look like as you scale your businesses?

Promotion means getting known. It's everything from telling a first date about your business when they ask you what you do for a living, all the way to appearing on a nationwide talk show, and anything in between. When I tell clients that they have to be more active in promoting themselves, they often struggle with where to start. What most business owners miss is that the best course of action is to first get crystal clear on what they want the promotion to accomplish, and then figure out the best vehicles for getting there.

For many of us, the problem is mental. Do you hold the limiting belief that you belong in the background? Do you secretly hold the assumption that you're not the person a customer should be moving forward with? Imposter syndrome making you question the insight you should be sharing? Are you apprehensive about promoting yourself because you're worried about what other people think about you?

Or maybe you're one of the over 70% of people who state that public speaking is their greatest fear. Getting clear on what your specific hang-up is the first step to overcoming it. The second is reminding yourself that you are doing this for your business and it's your responsibility as the leader to put yourself out there and get known. It won't be easy getting started, but if you truly believe in your brand proposition, lean on that to get you over the initial awkward hump of getting started. For me, the most powerful yet simple step was hitting the record button and doing it scared.

CREATIVITY FOLLOWS COMMITMENT

At our office, we say "creativity follows commitment". If you commit to posting on social media five times a day, you will suddenly become creative with your ideas in order to hit the target.

If you aren't clear about what you are committed to, the idea of content creation and promotion is this broad, abstract, and overwhelming idea. But locking in what you are exactly aiming for not only breaks the process up into manageable tasks; it also gives your creative juices a kick in the ass. Will you be cracking one-liners like a late-night talk host? Probably not, but you'll be surprised by how creative you become when you make the commitment to post.

You'll figure out how to talk about the vanilla shake that you're drinking: how it's tied to the massive sales you're having because it's the last one in the fridge. Or maybe there's a storm outside and you grab your phone to explain the water damage repair your roofing company offers. Your dog is asleep on the couch? Film it and say "You can have a nap because we will take care of X for you".

These are so simple-they're-stupid ideas – but they all work. That's what commitment does. It forces you to be creative about what's at your disposal in the here and now. I often do Instagram Live during my morning commute. I'm going to be in the car anyways, so it fulfills my need to promote without taking up extra time in my day. This gives me a chance to answer questions from followers about upcoming events and offerings, in between me thinking out loud to plan my day, and being frustrated about the guy who just cut me off. It works – people show up to watch them. I didn't go in with a big plan – I'm simply fulfilling my commitment to promote my business.

STARTING OUT

At its core, promotion is the act of getting attention. As you've been working on figuring out what to Stop, Start, Delegate, and Continue, start with a commitment to spend at least an hour a day on promotion. Start small, then build. The easiest thing to do right now is focus on the things that you can do with your phone. That's what I did. As your business gets bigger, you can be doing fancier production, but don't add complexity when you're first getting started. Get the discipline in first.

That hour a day that you start with should be nurtured to grow. Whatever mechanism – video, audio, written – you find works, keep showing up and paying attention to what works. Most people get so caught up in content planning for what they're doing tomorrow, next week, and next quarter that they spend more planning than promoting. Stop this. You don't need a fancy production and this big plan. Pick up your phone, hit record, and post. Just last night I recorded a TikTok about my meeting schedule. 45 seconds later, I went back into the app to delete it because

I thought it was dumb. I resisted the urge after I watched it and woke up this morning to find it has over 100k views. You never know what is going to work. Just stay committed.

BE YOURSELF

When you believe in what your organization is doing and what you have to offer, promotion becomes like second nature. The fundamental idea is that people don't want to do business with a robot. They want to connect and relate. I find my most impactful posts are ones that express my fears or honest thoughts on an upcoming situation.

Think of it like this: there are two accounting firms that you could be working with. Both are in the midst of a particularly brutal tax season. Key performers are running home to tuck in their kids, then returning to the office to keep working. Wearing jeans in the office on Sunday morning seems like a special treat. The first firm is posting stock images of smiling people shaking hands, saying platitudes like "We serve excellence" or "We go the extra mile for our clients". The second firm posts a video of one of their partners, standing in front of a dark window with bags under her eyes. "Hallelujah tax season is almost over!" She says, "We are so proud of our team for putting in long hours and serving our clients". Who'd you like to work with? Promotion is easy when you're just being yourself.

My husband released his book *9 Figure Mindset* in 2023, in which he unpacks his transformational framework for how we promote our business using the 7 Promotes. I'll give you the cliff notes but highly recommend you pick up a copy of his book to get more granular. First, Promote what you do. Second, Promote why you do it. Third, Promote who you do it for. Fourth, Promote the impact that somebody working with you should expect to receive (i.e., the value proposition). Fifth, Promote the benefits to those who choose to join your team and do it with you. Sixth, Promote your people to take over your roles so that you can work on your business. Seventh, Promote and teach everyone on your team to master the first six promotes!

WHEN TO STOP PROMOTING

How much promotion is enough promotion? How do you know when to stop? Whether you sell a product or service, it's likely that your deliverables have something finite about them. There comes a point where you could still be promoting even after your capacity to fulfill has been met. In that case, you should stop, right? At Cardone Ventures, we have a philosophy that you never stop promoting, even after you hit the target. These targets are usually quite fixed for us. So much of our work surrounds live events and there are only so many people we can get inside the venue at hand. But beyond getting butts in seats, we know that promotion continues to build energy. People tend to make a decision in the last few minutes, anyways.

We follow this principle, even when we have to "Suffer from success", as DJ Khaled would put it. Last year we oversold an event so significantly, that last minute we had to incur $67,000 of additional hotel, food, and beverage fees. On top of that, we had to call an audible to switch venues and locations due to how much we overshot our target for this event.

This cost us money, brought stress, and created chaos for our team – but we executed beautifully. We pulled together and did right by our customers. That event sparked our best month of Q3 last year. Moments like these rally the team. Your unwavering commitment pushes you to fulfill the big promises you've made. Never stop promoting.

The power of promoting is literally limitless. The important part to realize when it comes to promotion is you can do it. You've got this. And the reality is, you must start promoting as much as possible as often as possible. It's critical to your personal, professional, and financial success. As the leader of your business, you must get out there, evangelize your Vision and Mission, and demonstrate your Core Values whether you feel like it or not. On the other side, once you get past yourself and realize your promotion is a responsibility to your people, your company, and your purpose, you'll see some amazing things happen.

So pick up your phone, make a cringy video, and post it. Now. Start The Work.

*All the exclusive resources I mention in the book are ready for you to use, along with videos, tools, and extras that I couldn't share in this book, go to **StartTheWorkTools.com**.*

YOUR
CULTURE

- ☑ MISSION/VISION/CORE VALUES
- ☑ PROMOTION
- ☑ **ANNUAL PLANNING**
- ☐ QUARTERLY TEAM MEETINGS
- ☐ A HEALTHY MEETING CULTURE

CHAPTER 12

ANNUAL PLANNING

It's early January as I sit down to write this chapter. Brandon and I have just returned from Paris, where we were able to ring in the New Year and enjoy some welcomed time off away from the grind. One part celebration of the past, one part reflection on what the future can be, New Year's is one of my favorite holidays. This New Year was particularly memorable, not just because of the locale, but because it caps off our business' most successful year to date. From September through to Christmas, we've been elbow-deep in Annual Planning for 2024. We started with our revenue goals, worked out how we will hit them, and have a Resource Plan in place to hire the talent and resources we are going to need to pull it off. This has forced us to confront the challenges that we are going to encounter, taking care of them ahead of time so that we are able to hit the ground running.

This is a process we help implement with all of our clients called Annual Planning. Just like setting personal goals for the New Year allows us to imagine what's possible – the revenue target for your business should bring equal parts excitement and fear. You know Annual Planning is off to a great start when you look at your revenue goals for the coming year and ask "Is this really possible?"

Sean Stagnates Annual Planning process is simple. If anything, he sits down at the end of the year to project 10% growth on last year's numbers. The closest thing that he has to an annual team meeting is his Holiday party. Besides the fact that everyone is getting a couple weeks off for the holidays, there isn't much to celebrate from the mediocre year that has passed. Even if there was some success, Sean doesn't share it with his team: as far as he's concerned, he does everything himself and doesn't even have a core leadership team to help him. Even if he did have a year-end meeting, he questions the kind of impact, if any, it will have on the team.

Picture it, Sean Stagnates standing in front of the boardroom – his PowerPoint showing 5% growth from last year – and he's saying "Gee, I guess we can aim for 10% next year." He knows that's not really going to get anybody excited. In fact, he's worried that his team would almost be judgmental against him for holding the meeting. *"Sean's showing off,"* he thinks they'll say, *"his business made him 5% more last year, and our salaries stayed the same!"*

This anxiousness is in part because Sean has failed to offer Incentives for growth (which will be covered in Chapter 17), but also because he's spending too much time working in and not on his business. He doesn't feel like people are actually supporting him, so there's no reason to celebrate the last year or plan the next year collaboratively. Sean is destined for a year just like the last: one where he's juggling everything himself and not going anywhere. Why then have an Annual Planning process in place? Talking about the future means he'll have to answer the hard questions about today. He may even recall a time in the past when he went into a new year absolutely gung-ho as to how his business was going to excel. Maybe he was going to open up a new office to serve the next town over. Then January got busy and it wasn't until February that he realized he hadn't even started looking at real estate or preparing job posts for the new hires he'd have to make.

He never spent the time to assess what resources would be needed to accomplish his goals. This set him up to never actually go do these new things. He's been cynical about Annual Planning ever since. Let's crack open the process of Annual Planning and get you the tools you need to get your team on board for your best year yet. For the many of you who will be reading this book in the middle of the year, say the summer, don't worry. We'll cover how my methods of Annual Planning can be implemented for the start of the next business quarter.

ANNUAL PLANNING SCHEDULE

Ideally, Annual Planning isn't something that you just throw together in the craziness of December, much less in the first couple weeks of January. Your target should be to kick this process off a couple of months before the year even ends. This will give you the time it takes to create your targets, get your leadership team in alignment, and roll it out to everyone before the holidays so there's clarity come the first week of January.

The core components of Annual Planning are:

- Setting Revenue Targets
- Establishing Key Performance Indicator (KPI) Targets
- Resource Planning
- A Leadership Team Meeting
- An All-Team Meeting

The process of setting revenue targets takes place in September. This is when Brandon and I carve out time to discuss what's possible for the coming year – and what we need to do to progress along our greater, ten-year Vision for the business. Once the revenue target is defined, using the Revenue Algorithm discussed later in this chapter, I determine what KPI targets we need to hit in order to generate the targeted revenue. More on this to come in Chapter 16.

Once the Revenue and KPI targets are in place, the Resource Planning begins. Until we generated $50m in revenue, I was responsible for our Resource Planning – I didn't give the planning to the department heads as I knew who we needed and when in order to get our business to the next target. Most business owners should target rolling out a Department Budgeting process in the $15m-$20m range. If you think your Department Heads can properly forecast new hires based on targets, then by all means, delegate this responsibility to them but ensure you set proper expectations. It's likely your leaders have never done this before so they will inevitably ask for more new hires than you're able to pay for. Last year was actually the first year of rolling out Department Budgets and our team did in fact request many more hires than I approved. That's all part of the fun. Don't be surprised when this happens.

You might be asking "How do I know how many new hires to approve?" Use $350,000 to $500,000 of revenue per employee as your guide. If you're a $15m company, you should not have more than 30 to 42 employees. If you do, you're not as profitable as you should be and have likely structured your team to have less output than what's optimal. If your target for next year is $20m, the math would look like this: $20,000,000 (targeted revenue) divided by $500,000 (revenue per employee target) = 40 employees. If you currently have 35 employees, you'd be approving 5 new hires for the upcoming year. Choose wisely.

In October, bring in your leadership team. If you're having them help with Resource Planning, this should kick off early October through sending them their Department budgets and having them fill in their resource requests based on the revenue targets you've already established. You'll be hosting a Leadership Team Annual Planning session in mid-late October to unveil next year's plan and get everyone on the same page. This flows nicely into November, which is when we do Performance Reviews at Cardone Ventures. This is when you assess where the team is at and solidify their goals and opportunities for the year to come. In these reviews, take note and give direct feedback on where they excel and where they need improvement. My full Performance Review process is laid out in *TeamWork* and includes all the forms and email templates I use across all of our businesses.

After the initial Annual Plan that's developed from September to October is distilled through these different layers, it comes time to put it all together (with end-of-year numbers that are almost fully materialized) for our Annual Team meeting in December. We have Quarterly Team Meetings 3 times a year and the meeting in December serves as our Annual Team Meeting because we share the targets and objectives for the following year.

BUILDING AROUND REVENUE TARGETS

When it comes to choosing annual revenue targets, there is a formula. You shouldn't be guessing. You also shouldn't be just picking a random number above what you did last year. My husband has told me stories about how he used to sit through hundreds of hours a year with executive teams all sitting around the table spending 90 days "formulating" annual budgets in his public companies and all those targets or budgets were never hit. Every quarter he would sit in meetings with executives explaining how they needed to "forward invest", "pull forward" spending, and move targets to "end of year catch up". He vowed to never run any business like this. Instead of a complicated process that involved "professionals", he came up with the structure I'm about to walk you through that removes weeks of planning and simplifies the complexity. This process will empower your team to spend their energy on how to create programs and promotions to actually hit the agreed on targets. I just want to remind you that irrespective of what your accounting "professionals" tell you, we have successfully started, built, and sold multiple businesses from scratch. My husband exited his last business for 77x EBITDA and in just the past four and a half years, we've formatted over two and a half billion in businesses using this concept below. It can be done in one hour and free up yours and your team's time to focus on how to hit these targets. To simplify a traditionally complicated and over engineered process, this is how we set budgets and revenue targets.

To start, there should be three numbers in your head when going into a new year: the low, medium, and high targets. To get these, we use this Revenue Algorithm:

- **Low Target:** Add your top 3 months of Revenue over the past 12 months, divide by 3, and multiply by 12. Let's create an example: Sally Scale's top 3 months of revenue last year were $92,000, $101,000, and $124,000. So let's add them together ($317,000) and divide by 3 months to get the monthly target ($105,666.67). Now let's take the monthly target of $105,000 and multiply by 12 months to get the annual revenue target of $1,268,000.

- **Medium Target:** Take your top revenue month over the past 12 months and multiply by 12. In Sally's case, we'd be taking her best month of $124,000 and multiplying it by 12 months to get us an annual revenue target of $1,488,000.

- **High Target:** Take your top revenue month over the past 12 months and multiply by 12. The recommended growth rate depends on your commitment to your goals. In Sally's case, we're going to use a 50% growth rate as she's looking to expand to a new location next year. So using the $1,488,000 target from the Medium Target, we're going to multiply it by .5 to get us $744,000 in additional revenue. Let's add the $1,488,000 to $744,000 to get the High Target of $2.232,000.

How should you be using these three targets?

Aim high. Budget low. We set all of our KPIs around our High Target and that's the number we share during the Annual Planning rollout to the team. We use the Low Target to establish our expenses and resource planning for next year. If you resource plan around the Low Target, you won't accidentally overspend while chasing after your High Target.

The High Target allows you to have a lofty and ultimate goal for the year, while the Low Target allows your accounting team to have a clear number to calibrate the budget around. This keeps you from overextending your capital and resource investments. This is going to be a card you'll play close to the chest. You don't want the majority of your team to even know that this number exists. The Low Target only exists to inform how you are going to budget for the year.

In the best-case scenario when your team blows by this Low Target, there is room for reforecasting. In a worst-case scenario, you're sitting comfortably with a budget that doesn't outkick the coverage. An important thing to remember: this Low Target isn't something to scoff at. It's the average of your best three months the prior year. Being able to replicate the best your business can be in all twelve months should still create a benchmark year for your organization. Whether you hit the High or Low Target, your business will still have scaled – expect nothing less when you put in the work to plan the growth of your organization.

Imagine if you were a math teacher, trying to get the most out of your students. Would you stand in front of the class and tell them it takes a 60% to pass, or would you encourage them by saying you think they can all hit 90% and beyond?

The same logic applies to how you're going to share revenue targets with your team. While the Low Target goes to the expense protectors in your business who are accounting for costs, the revenue generators should be given the High Target.

To your sales team, there should only be one milestone to hit: Excellence. Getting people to buy into your vision for what's quantifiably possible in a year is equal parts motivation and pressure. A massive goal leaves you and your team with a massive problem: once you have it, it's time to figure out how it's going to happen.

KPI TARGETS

When we think abstractly about growth – be it personal, professional, or financial – we can get overwhelmed with the sea of possibilities. So how do you parse through all the opportunities and prioritize what's most crucial to pursue in this new year? You start by looking at what you want the year's outcome to be, so you get the luxury of working backward to determine the "how" for your annual goals. You can't do it all – and you don't have to. If there are multiple ways that you could be scaling and you haven't gotten clear on the outcome you are looking for, you run the risk of chasing everything at once and losing direction. But with a tangible revenue target in your mind, all you're doing is slotting in opportunities for expansion like they are puzzle pieces. This will move you towards knowing the exact mechanism for growth within your business.

A business can expand and add revenue in only a handful of ways:

1) Acquiring more customers to buy your existing products/services

2) Increasing the price of existing products/services

3) Adding new locations

4) Adopting new products/services

5) Buying a connected business

Think of Sarah Scales and her dental practice. Once she's clear on her revenue growth goals, in her case 120%, she can sleuth out the best vehicles for her business to get there. Expanding her patient base is the obvious suspect, but she rules it out: her current location doesn't have any more operatories for extra appointments and the calendar is already booked out months in advance. Maybe she could hit 10% growth if she really squeezed it, but this won't cut it. Increasing the price of services won't do it either, that would price out her ideal customer. What Sarah's left with is the conviction that a new location is needed. Because the growth is going to come from an acquisition, guess what Sarah now needs to spend time doing? Searching for a business to buy! This would be added to her "Start" activities, which puts all the more emphasis on getting her current processes documented and duplicated so she'll have the time to do site visits and meet with potential acquisition targets.

You can't get clear on how your business is going to grow until you hone in on what you want the outcome to be. In the same way, the outcome you want is empty until it's backed up with the plan for how it will materialize. This puts some meat behind the initial targets that you've calculated. When you go to present these numbers to your team, you won't just be somebody with a crazy vision, you'll be a leader with a plan. In nailing down the outcomes you're after and how you will reach them, you make the idea of scaling tangible. Instead of setting abstract expectations for your team, everyone will be clear on how things will grow.

Take off the boss hat and imagine yourself as a salesperson. Think about being asked to generate $1,500,000 in new business over the course of the next year. To most people, that's overwhelming. But what if you were presented with a graph that breaks down the types of packages that will have to be sold and the campaigns that will be run with corresponding targets for every month of the year?

You can – to great effect – break your revenue target down into monthly and weekly goals. Being that specific is going to help you execute when the time comes instead of missing the opportunity because you weren't paying attention and clear on your target. Specificity makes goals attainable and clear for your team and this is the purpose of KPIs (Chapter 16 dives into this fully). Do not neglect the "how" behind everything you want out of the next year. Before you bring the plan to the team, however, one more thing remains to be determined: "who" you are going to need.

RESOURCE PLANNING

This is arguably the most intricate part of the Annual Planning process – think of it like looking into a crystal ball to see what you will need from vendors, employees, investments, and technology in order to hit your stated revenue target.

Let's imagine that you plan on adding a new product this year. When you get into what needs to happen to accomplish this, you'll realize that means increasing the number of vendors you have to diversify your inventory. As you think about this, you remember how fragmented your current vendor management is, as it's managed by individual people. To increase the amount of vendors, you're going to have to find someone to consolidate this and get the new vendors organized.

Sitting down to work out what you need to fuel the mechanisms for growth in your business allows you to create a clear picture of what is to come. This is going to help your team with budgeting: you're able to look at your revenue goal and assess what additional resources are needed to hit your goal. Because of this, this stage in the process is going to be heavily informed by both the high and low revenue targets.

What does this look like? Let's take hiring for example.

Imagine that you need to grow your sales team by 4 people in order to hit your high target. If you make these hires now, you have who you need to scale your business, but you've just hired for growth that you don't currently have. When you're in Annual Planning, it's not about going out and doing what you think needs to happen right away. You're not hiring now but are you prepared for when you are ready (like having job descriptions, onboarding plans, and metrics to set the new hire up for success?) Your target is to be prepared instead of reactionary.

You've budgeted around the low target, so it's best to not implement anything that goes beyond it until your target becomes a reality. This stage of Annual Planning is about preparing these moves so that they can be enacted at the drop of a hat. My target is to have a fully laid out Resource Plan by the start of the year. This plan tells me which months I will need new hires, and which roles, as we hit our revenue targets. This way, at the beginning of each month when I sit down to review the financial performance from the previous month, I can quickly assess where our revenue is at in relation to our budget and approve or push off posting for the targeted new roles based on the results. This type of organization prevents you from being reactionary when you start adding the long-awaited revenue you've been working hard to generate. Most business owners, like our friend Sean Stagnates, get excited but instantly panic when the new revenue target hits, because he didn't think through what needs to happen next to scale with the revenue. Luckily, you aren't like Sean and already had everything in place including the job posts, Onboarding Plan, and Tell Me, Show Me, Let Me, Coach Me training in place.

ANNUAL PLANNING LEADERSHIP TEAM MEETING

The important thing to remember going into your Leadership Team meeting is that you should have a strong sense of all three elements discussed earlier in the chapter – Revenue Targets, KPI Targets, and your Resource Plan – before you start meeting with your team. As needed, you can lean on the expertise of finance and accounting, but the goals will come from you. When you go to your team – top to bottom – remember that you're not polling them or asking their opinion on what the goals should be for the coming year. The moment you do that is when it all falls apart. Having too many cooks in the kitchen will create a plan that has no direction and is not clear on the outcomes being pursued. When you're presenting the team with the vision for the coming year, it's past the point of debate. Meeting with them is about rolling out the plan and casting your expectations for each department.

The collaboration part comes in discussions on what needs to be overcome in order to achieve these goals. This is where your team gets to share the challenges they see standing in the way of this new vision. This is why we start the Annual Planning process early, so we have November and December to iron out these kinks and start the new year ready to go.

This is the exact email I sent our Leadership team this year to get them ready for our Annual Planning Leadership Team Meeting:

PREP EMAIL

TO:

SUBJECT: Annual Planning

Hey Team,

It's that time - Annual Planning for next year is right around the corner! In order to be prepped and ready for our meeting later this month, please dedicate 1 hour between now and then to prep, document, and able to share the items below in our Annual Planning Leadership Team Meeting.

Annual Planning Prep:

- What personal win are you most proud of from this year?
- What is your intention for our Annual Planning Meeting?
- What topic do you want to ensure we discuss during this meeting?
- What departmental win are you most proud of from this year?
- Prepare a Department SWOT Analysis
- NEXT YEAR'S PERSONAL OBJECTIVES: What are the 3-5 strategic Objectives you need to focus on in next year to hit the established Targets?
- Q1 PERSONAL OBJECTIVES : What are the 3-5 strategic Objectives you need to focus on Q1 to hit the established Targets?
- NEXT YEAR'S DEPARTMENT OBJECTIVES : What are the 5-7 strategic Objectives your Department needs to focus on next to hit the established Targets?
- Q1 DEPARTMENT OBJECTIVES : What are the 3-5 strategic Objectives your Department needs to focus on Q1 to hit the established Targets?

Looking forward to creating the future with you!

Sincerely,
Natalie

When you're having these discussions with the different departments of your business, it's good to have a framework that you can lean on. Ours, like many organizations, uses SWOT analysis in situations like these: Strengths, Weaknesses, Opportunities, and Threats. SWOT separates internal and external factors, with Strengths and Weaknesses describing the former and Opportunities and Threats being the latter. This is also useful to pull up the coming quarters to assess if the Department head made progress on the Opportunities, Weaknesses, and Threats. Their progress, or lack thereof, should be highlighted during their Performance Review.

This Leadership Team Meeting is one of the best meetings of the year. We take an entire day to unveil the targets and strategic areas of growth and then go through each department's prep document to get our team communicating about cross-departmental and systemic issues we need to address in order for us to achieve the stated targets. Many companies go offsite for this meeting – if you can, you should. It's an important time to have everyone's attention on strategy instead of the day-to-day minutia. This meeting should be the catalyst for your team to identify where they need to spend their time in the last quarter of the year to get ready for the year ahead.

ALL TEAM ANNUAL MEETING

All this comes together for the All Team Annual meeting. This is not just a fuzzy-feel-good-end-of-year get together that you're putting on for shits and giggles. This is you making commitments and creating your company's future results. This is why it's so crucial to have the ins and outs of your presentation thought out. You're not sharing a dream. The details of how you are going to be scaling the company should be so concrete that it feels like they've already happened.

Start with the outcome – the High Target – that you've established for the next year. Half sexy, half scary, you'll get both their attention and their doubts. Then show how it will be done, in the form of measurable KPIs, so that every department (and individual within) knows exactly what role they have to play in that overall goal. This should be shown as the Organizational KPIs for the year and then broken down into the Organizational KPIs for Q1. This is where you're driving the team's attention. What do they have control over? Q1.

Have you kept every single one of your New Year's resolutions? Likely, no. Sticking with the targets, expectations, and tasks laid out in Annual Planning takes discipline. My advice is to refer back to your Annual Plan targets often. Have your targets – and how they are to be achieved – organized into a spreadsheet that's readily available to you as a touchstone. This gets reported to me weekly – I suggest you do the same. Just like your personal New Year's resolutions, you fail them only when you forget them. Avoiding failure requires discomfort.

If you are committed to going from 200 to 160 pounds in a year, reminding yourself of this goal means that you are committed to standing on the scale every day. If you are looking to save more, you can't avoid looking at your credit card statement because ignorance is bliss. In the same vein, when you set KPI targets at the start of the year, you have to check them, risking the discomfort of seeing something that needs drastic improvements. If you've broken it down well enough, you should be able to check what the monthly and weekly targets are. This makes the big overall numbers more applicable to the here-and-now and manageable.

While we're on the topic of how Annual Planning informs how you should act throughout the year, let's think about what you can do if you're reading this in the middle of the summer (and are realizing that you could've planned this year better).If you are reading this and don't want to wait until the end of the year to try out this process, you're in luck. The theory and practices discussed in this chapter can be applied to quarters. Target the closest quarterly start. If it's currently May, kick this off in July at the start of Q3. Share the outcomes of what happened in the last quarter. State your well-defined Revenue and KPI targets for the next 6 months. It's not complicated, like many of the elements of scaling a business, you just have to see its importance and be diligent about it. This can even be a great practice round for the big Annual Planning session that is to come. It was none other than Ben Franklin – the man on the $100 bill – who said "By failing to prepare, you are preparing to fail".

As you can tell, I'm passionate when it comes to Annual Planning. There's a strong mix of emotion and logic that goes into setting targets, mapping out a strategy, and having the courage to commit to the unknown. Yet it's exactly what's required to get the most out of your promotion, your people, and your processes. Without it, chaos ensues, and scaling becomes impossible. This book is to help you start the work to scale successfully. Without the attention to detail required to make smart goals for the year, you leave your people and your business drifting aimlessly along in day-to-day activities, with no destination and no way to measure success. This is a recipe for disaster, so lean into the intensity and possibilities that come with a strong Annual Planning process. Your future business and your future self will be truly grateful you took the time to start the work, establishing what to Start, Continue, Delegate, and Stop on a macro level to support doing the same on the micro level.

All the exclusive resources I mention in the book are ready for you to use, along with videos, tools, and extras that I couldn't share in this book, go to **StartTheWorkTools.com**.

YOUR
CULTURE

- ☑ MISSION/VISION/CORE VALUES
- ☑ PROMOTION
- ☑ ANNUAL PLANNING
- ☑ **QUARTERLY TEAM MEETINGS**
- ☐ A HEALTHY MEETING CULTURE

CHAPTER 13

QUARTERLY TEAM MEETINGS

Quarterly team meetings (we'll call them QTMs for short) – are a crucial investment in the success of your organization. I know, I know – this doesn't sound like the best use of your time. But, if it's not already, you should be adding QTMs to your Start list. Trust me, this is worth your time.

QTMs function as a linchpin for cohesive teamwork – aligning strategies, tactics, and actions within your organization. Without this synchronized understanding, organizational growth is at risk, and the absence of QTMs will lead to a communication void. This is a recurring opportunity for leadership to communicate pivotal, company-wide changes. It instills confidence in your team regarding the company's trajectory and equips them with actionable steps for immediate implementation. It's all based on a very simple philosophy: you need your entire organization to be on the same page – moving in lockstep from their respective corners – as the business grows. When the business grows without this cross-departmental understanding, without the focus on seeing how your strategies, tactics, and actions are interrelated, you run the risk of growing and falling apart.

Take this seriously – an intentionally crafted and thought-out plan is essential. View these sessions as a strategic investment in the cohesion, direction, and ultimate success of your organization. In *TeamWork*, I walk you through my tried-and-true agenda that's broken down by Cultural, Operational, and Financial integration. I highly recommend you pick up a copy of *TeamWork* and use the same agenda. For this book, I want to dive deeper into what you need to focus on during your first QTM and give you some tips on how to make them run smoothly.

Before kicking off your first QTM, the resounding question you should be asking yourself is "What do people need to know?" This isn't a time to share with the whole company your new hare-brained ideas that aren't core to the business – it's the time to share the vision and create clarity on the actionable priorities for the next 3 months. Because these meetings take place quarterly, this helps you stay focused on keeping the main thing the main thing. You should not be discussing "potential partners" or "maybes". This agenda should create a straightforward roadmap of what to expect in the coming 3 months.

Now for your first one, it's helpful to provide an org chart if you haven't had one shared with the team before. Organization (Org) charts provide structure and give team members an understanding of departments and roles inside your business. Word to the wise: make sure it's correct and triple-check it before kicking off your meeting. I recently had an experience where I left an important role off of the org chart and the whole team saw it. Is it the worst mistake? No. However, it's not a good thing to do and your team members want to know that you see them and value them. Even though you know it was an oversight, it should be your intention to make sure it's updated and correct.

My philosophy for sharing updates and information with our entire company is radical transparency. If we're off target, it's not the time to sugarcoat or leave out that information. Especially as you grow and develop your leaders, the more you demand transparency and accountability, the better these meetings go. This is not a rah-rah meeting – it's a time to get the whole company on the same page regarding the state of the organization and what they can do to help get it to the next level. Only reporting on the good things and not acknowledging the losses creates a fluffy culture. Fluff doesn't get results – being direct and taking action does. I encourage you to stick true to sharing real Metrics, the good and the bad, so that the team is empowered and understand what they can do to help.

We have a saying that "The only emotion allowed in business is celebration". Sometimes these meetings don't exactly share results that are worth celebrating. When you're not hitting your numbers, this meeting can feel like a dread, and you will likely consider scrapping it altogether. The quarters you are off are the exact opportunities that the quarterly team meeting is built for. This meeting forces you and the team to confront where the business is at and come up with a plan. It's not easy but think through your alternatives. Are you going to decide to hide that things aren't going well? Fix it yourself? Pretend it doesn't exist? None of these are great options. Your best chance of being successful is through sharing the missed targets with the team you've hired to help you and focus everybody on what can be done.

In the first quarter of 2021, we were off from our target by 37%, and you could feel the heaviness during the meeting. It's painful to fumble out of the gate when you have big plans for the year. The meeting was myopically focused on the three KPIs we needed to focus on to make up for the bad quarter in the next one. There was clarity, and every team knew what they needed to do to close the gap. In Q2, we entirely made up the 37% from Q1 and ended up being 11% over target. That quarter, the meeting was electric! The energy was palpable and the team celebrated.

After the meeting, I called our exec team to congratulate them on an incredible quarter. Each of them commented on how incredible the meeting was and how excited their teams were.

The next day, I got a resignation from a team member who had been with us for two weeks. She said that we expected too much, and this wasn't a "cultural" fit for her. My response? If hitting our company's goals so that our teams accomplish their goals isn't a cultural fit for her: good riddance.

You should create the framework by kicking-off and closing the meeting. The majority of the content should be driven by your leaders. Resist the urge to be the one talking the whole time. Your team will take more responsibility when you give it to them. Even if they do not deliver the message in the same way you would or use the perfect analogy you had in your head to drive a point home, let them take the lead and give feedback after. I start the deck creation for our QTMs 3 weeks before the scheduled date. In each section, I tag the team members who I am assigning to populate the data and give them a deadline of a week out from the meeting. Once the deadline comes, it gives me a chance to review each slide and meet with any leader who didn't complete it properly or added something that hadn't been agreed upon. Let them take a stab at the content, but at the end of the day, you have ultimate accountability for the success of the meeting. I've made the mistake of trusting my leaders and not verifying the information they added to the deck just to show up and hear about a new idea, that I'm not aligned with, for the first time with all of our team on the call. No bueno. Trust but verify.

Most of these meetings happen virtually these days with the clients I work with as it allows for the meeting to run smoothly and be recorded for future training. I recommend having new employees watch last quarter's QTM during their onboarding. It will catch them up to speed quickly on how the organization operates and what they should be focusing on. Having it virtually also allows you to send it to anyone who might be out of the office during the scheduled time. I remember in the early 2010's when we would go off site each quarter for these meetings. It was difficult to keep the energy high and get through the important items. It felt more like a speech than an update – this is why I'm a big fan of virtual QTMs even if your team all works onsite.

Doing it for the first time can feel difficult. The energy might be low and you likely won't have people calling and emailing you afterwards to tell you how amazing it was. This can feel like a downer because you've put all of this hard work into it without much of a response. That's okay. Think of this meeting like a discipline. You do it because it's the right thing to do for your team and your business. You do it to know that you thoughtfully put a plan together. When it's over, I recommend sending a video message to your leaders who participated to congratulate and thank them. They were likely nervous and prepared diligently for their time in the spotlight. As the leader, it's okay that no one thanks you even when you feel like someone should be patting you on the back. That's your role as a leader. Know that I'm here cheering you on and proud that you did it!

Once the meeting has concluded, you should upload the deck and the video recording to a shared place where team members can access it and new team members can review during onboarding. A nice follow up email to the team reiterating the main 2 or 3 points never hurt either. The more energy you inject into this initiative, the quicker it will catch on and become a norm inside your business. Once this tactical stuff is handled, give yourself a ranking on the following questions:

1) On a scale of 1-5, how inspirational was the meeting?

2) On a scale of 1-5, how engaged was the team during the meeting?

3) On a scale of 1-5, how accurate was the information?

4) What do you need to change for next time?

Be honest and give yourself actionable feedback. These meetings should iterate and get better as time goes on. If you were the only one commenting in the chat, follow up with your leaders about how they can be better at participating. If you noticed people on their phones or doing work, add a slide to the beginning next time to set expectations. I promise that this won't be amazing the first time you do it but the only way to get better is to make tweaks based on what didn't work.

This is one of the most highly leverageable ways for you to spend your time. It takes 3 to 4 hours of planning to align all of your team on the cultural, operational, and financial priorities for your business over the next 3 months. If you don't implement this, ask yourself "Where and how do people get this information?" Without a QTM, your leaders are playing a game of broken telephone, the passing of information gets more and more watered down as it's relayed from person to person.

Transparency – whether you crush targets, or miss them – is essential to keeping your culture rallying around your vision. The QTM is your time to set the example, to recalibrate your people, and show how all of their hard work is contributing to the bigger picture – and impacting the lives of your clients and customers. Take accountability for the alignment of your culture and Start The Work.

All the exclusive resources I mention in the book are ready for you to use, along with videos, tools, and extras that I couldn't share in this book, go to
StartTheWorkTools.com.

YOUR
CULTURE

- ☑ MISSION/VISION/CORE VALUES
- ☑ PROMOTION
- ☑ ANNUAL PLANNING
- ☑ QUARTERLY TEAM MEETINGS
- ☑ **A HEALTHY MEETING CULTURE**

CHAPTER 14

A HEALTHY MEETING CULTURE

Sean Stagnates runs his meetings off the cuff. There isn't a rhyme or rhythm to anything. A few jokes, followed by an impromptu review of the day's schedule, maybe a daily stand-up where everyone's too shy to speak up. Wrap it up with some awkward small talk. Then Sean and company are off to the races for another day of stagnant business. There's no structure to Sean's meetings. On days where he can't make it to the office, the meeting can't be replicated, because there is no framework *to* replicate. If you think the meeting is a waste of time when Sean's around, you should see things when he isn't. Any attempts to duplicate the presence of this free-wheeling boss are nothing but an unproductive drain on company time and resources.

On the contrary, Sarah Scales wields meetings like they're her greatest weapon (because they are). This is one of the fundamental reasons her business is scaling quickly. The awesome part is this: while it's important for Sarah to show up for her team, things are set up in a way that they can run without her (when they need to). There's a structure to each one of her dental practice's meetings. They're transparent, every team member knows it well enough that they can lead the meetings in her absence. There's room for sharing wins, but each one gets to the priorities quickly and efficiently – because everyone knows what the meeting needs to cover before the meeting even takes place.

Sarah has created a healthy meeting culture. She and her team have leveraged this culture into a highly effective tool for not only maintaining but also scaling her business.

She's crafted a formula for meetings that reliably:

- Don't waste Sarah's time
- Don't waste her team's time
- Contain valuable decisions that impact growth
- Document what decisions are being made

KEEPING ORGANIZED

Inside my business, there are hundreds of decisions being made every day. Most of these have a short and long-term impact on how we do business. As we continue to scale, these decisions compound and our leaders (including myself) lose the ability to recall off the top of their heads when, why, or by whom a particular decision was made or where the initiative left off. It may seem silly to you now, but we have times when one of our executives will be completely fed up with a certain process that's been in place for months. They start going off in a meeting about the bad process and try to uncover who made such an inefficient process. Yet, they've forgotten that they were the one that personally suggested it in the first place. That's the rate of scaling that we're talking about in this book.

You should be able to easily get clarity, hold decision-makers accountable, and preserve the reasoning behind every decision. This is all made possible in the way that you plan, execute, and follow up on your meetings.

CONTAINERS FOR CONVERSATIONS

Meetings are containers for all of the ideas and decisions that shape the growth of your business. Understanding the replicable framework for a good meeting will create the optimal environment for value-driving decisions that fuel your growth.

Meetings are your best friend. As you scale and become further removed from hands-on work, they will serve as touchstones for you to remain connected to elements of your organization that need your attention. They will maintain your presence in all things while leaving a healthy separation for departments to run smoothly without you. What hurts many business leaders is that they don't have a framework for their meetings. They schedule meetings when something is on fire and needs to be discussed immediately. Their day is a barrage of one firefighting meeting to the next so everything feels random and chaotic. Thinking of your meetings as containers to hold important conversations is a helpful concept to get you started.

Imagine if your favorite restaurant down the street had never standardized its takeout containers. When you ordered in, the delivery driver would come with food packed into whatever could be found in the kitchen. Some of the containers overflow with food, pasta sauce oozes from under the lid, and noodles fly everywhere when you open it up. But your dessert, the slice of cherry pie, that's been placed in the biggest container. It had so much extra space that it got sloshed around in transit and is now ruined. Are your meetings the right containers for the conversations you need to have? Are they too full? Are they too empty? Above all, are they replicable? Let's break down how to create a healthy meeting culture – so every key conversation can be properly contained. In the downloadable (available at *StartTheWorkTools.com*), you'll find my list of recurring meetings and some special bonus content on how I make them run efficiently. Let's dive into how to set up your meetings for success.

MEETING PREP

All my meetings – from weekly Executive meetings to One-on-Ones – are blocked out in my calendar. If I were to click on a meeting on my calendar, I have an option to open up the agenda for the meeting. This is a standardized spreadsheet template that holds the agenda for that meeting. Everybody who is coming to the meeting has access to the agenda. They are expected to add any items they want to discuss or need clarity before the meeting. That way, there are no surprises, and we can all prepare to respond to each matter at hand effectively.

Meetings waste time when you and your team fail to prepare. Do your meetings continue to block out more space than is needed? Do they often become overloaded with additional topics that pop up sporadically? When you require an agenda ahead of time, these problems disappear. Before starting my day, I'm checking the agenda of the meetings I'm attending. If the agenda is longer than the time we have to meet, I can proactively book time for a secondary meeting, or account for the likelihood that we're going to at least run a few minutes long.

If I do not see much activity on the agenda and there isn't anything important to decide – I cancel and pull the plug on the meeting. There should be no meetings for meeting's sake. Implement a system for planning an agenda ahead of time and you will be able to say the same.

You are leading a business. That business will be growing quickly. The value of your time will grow exponentially and so will your team's need to have reliable access to your executive decision-making. If something comes up for a member of my team on a Tuesday and they know that they're in a meeting with me on Thursday – they can add it to the agenda for that meeting. Our meeting culture is set up in a way that everyone has a timeline for when important matters can be discussed and acted upon. This keeps me from getting my phone blown up for all matters big and small throughout the day.

I was working with a business owner who was struggling to get important work done because there was always a line of people waiting outside her door to ask her a question when she had a moment to spare. She went on and on about how everything is always on fire until I asked her "When would you recommend to them that they get those answers from you?" It hadn't dawned on her that she created this issue because she wasn't thinking strategically – she was in the weeds. What she learned and what you need to know is your meeting culture is the product of two things: a tool and an expectation.

The tool is the process for agenda-setting. The expectation is that it is being used. The thing holding so many business leaders back from growth is that they're going through the motions and repeating tired and purposeless meetings that accomplish nothing because there is no preparation and there is no accountability. Agenda setting takes you and your team mere minutes and will save you hours.

A great meeting is dictated both by the agenda and the attendees. Edit meticulously who is in each meeting. Everything comes down to what people need to know and what they need to contribute. I'm constantly editing who is in what meeting. If I see that 2 out of 7 people are primarily driving the conversation 2 weeks in a row, I'll ask them to set up their own meeting and report back on next actions. I also have no fear of kicking people out of meetings who don't need to be there. We recently had a leadership team member who would show up to every meeting but hadn't said anything or added an agenda item for a month. I pulled him aside and said if he doesn't have anything to contribute, why is he there? You're not paying for people to be in meetings – you're paying for an outcome. Meetings, especially leadership meetings, can sometimes make people feel important. Nip that in the bud and only reward people who achieve results. Being "busy" from being in meetings all week is not a reason to not produce. It's your job to teach that to your leaders.

I also just coached a leader in one of our departments on saying "no" to meetings. She was struggling to keep up with her work and when I looked at her calendar, it was filled from morning to night with meetings. No wonder she wasn't able to move things forward – she was busy all day! I let her know that she needed to block time each day for the work she needed to do and gave her permission to say "no" to things that didn't need her. She thanked me afterward because she didn't know that she could say "no". I can't emphasize enough how important it is for you to figure out how to prepare for and set up your time so that you can help your team do the same. If you can't figure out how to get out of meetings and create structure, you will not be able to help your team when they have the same struggles.

DURING THE MEETING

When you have the agenda laid out before the fact, meetings become useful and straightforward to run. It's simply a matter of bringing up the topics in the Agenda until all the necessary information has been shared and decisions have been made. I had a last-minute opportunity in January last year to fly from Miami to Paris on a trip with Vogue. The opportunity came on a Wednesday and I was supposed to leave for a week 4 days later. I said yes with little hesitation because even though I couldn't be in all of the meetings I had scheduled, the show could go on without me because I structured it that way.

The Vogue opportunity was exactly the opportunity I had been hoping for 11 months. I had been preparing our organization to allow me to not be in the day-to-day. When this opportunity came, I was ready. I was able to stay up to speed by reading the Agendas and Next Actions from the meetings I missed and followed up on a handful of items that needed my attention. And guess what? The business continued to grow and we doubled from the previous January. This is the goal!

So much of a well-run meeting is in the set-up, but I do have a very specific framework for taking notes on the Agenda during each meeting

NOTE TAKING

I recommend having two types of templates that you use with your team depending on the type of meeting you're having. One for Next Actions Notes and one for Meeting Recap Notes. I learned this from one of my early mentors – she was the CTO at the company I worked for and a total boss. She influenced all of the operating decisions in the company and had a real impact on meetings she attended. I looked up to her and wanted to emulate her because of the influence she had. She taught me that I needed to get good at taking down the Next Action Notes for everything that was talked about. These notes are taken based on the Agenda for the meeting and predominantly focused on the Next Actions for each Agenda item.

However, her superpower and influence came in her ability to distill information in the larger, more nebulous meetings – those were the important ones. On longer meetings, those with looser Agendas, cross-departmental, or with new vendors/partners to explore an idea, just recording Next Actions is not enough. You need a place to organize all of the conversation taking place so you don't waste your time flying to a city with a group of people, spending 4 hours talking, and leaving without clarity on what was said, what needs to happen, and by when. This is where the Meeting Recap is invaluable.

I break up these types of notes into the following categories:

NEXT ACTION NOTES

Using the Agenda, Next Action Notes put down the clearly defined next action, along with the name of the person who is accountable. As you see in the Agenda Visual, the first column is the Agenda Item. The second column is Lead who added this topic to the Agenda. The third column is for the Next Actions. The best format for a Next Action is starting it with the person's name, adding the next action, and then ending it with the due date. An example would be: Jeremy G – Call the client to share the next paid traffic strategy – 5/12. The Notes column is for any additional information that might be useful to reference or share with your team.

MEETING AGENDA

AGENDA ITEM	LEAD	NEXT ACTIONS	NOTES
Annual Planning	Natalie	Natalie: Send out Prep packet	Provide status update and plan for how departments will work together.
VIP Client Dinner	Kandis	Kandis: Follow up with Events team on seating arrangement	Seating arrangement, client communication, team expecations
Influencer Event Logistics	Deric	Deric: Reach out to clients by end of day 12/3	
Partnership Contract Updates	Ashley	Ashley: Update the Process Tracker	
Process For Promotion Within	Natalie	Natalie: Update the Leadership team on the changes to the Process for Promotion within	What is the process if we think someone internal would be a good fit for a different role?
Clients & Service Contract/ Extended Warranty Opportunities	Deric	Deric: Set up calls with the 6 clients by 12/6	Facilitated successful meeting with team and vendor to discuss service contract/extended warranty opportunities across the portfolio. Immediate opportunities with 6 targeted clients.

When the agenda item is being discussed, it's critical to capture what is happening to move this item forward and highlight when it needs to be done. The timeline is the most important part! This is usually where people create confusion in meetings. Everyone is clear on what needs to happen next but one person thinks it's getting handled by the end of the day and the other person thinks it's due at the end of the month. Clear this up before the meeting ends. If the problem gets resolved and there's no one responsible for doing anything with the item, I highly recommend still adding the context of the decision in this column for reference. This helps bring anyone up to speed who wasn't at the meeting and can also be useful in the future when time has passed and no one recalls what happened with the initiative.

MEETING RECAP NOTES

Meeting Name: _____

Attendees: _____

Date: _____

DISCUSSION	
DECISIONS	
QUESTIONS	
NEXT STEPS	

ATTENDEES

This is fairly self-explanatory: record who was in the room/on the call. If this meeting is with new people, I write down names, titles, and anything important they share in their intro so that I can remember the context. I use this note taking format heavily with new relationships that we vet. Otherwise, it's all too easy to just hop right into the opportunity and forget to get the context of who the stakeholders are and identify their roles.

DISCUSSION

This is where I take my loose notes as the conversation flows. They're often messy and disorganized at first. My goal with this section is to capture the topics that were covered in the meeting that I will want to remember after we're done. You should be able to send this to an internal team member who missed the meeting to catch them up to speed quickly on the important highlights. This isn't documenting every detail – it's following the main points and brief context for each.

DECISIONS

In less structured meetings, lots of small decisions can be made without everyone noticing. This category is to capture what those decisions were so that everyone is clear afterward on what was decided. There shouldn't be any action items with these bullets, if there is an action item, it should be placed under Next Steps. When these decisions are made in meetings, writing them down helps you disseminate this data to others who weren't present and are impacted by the decisions.

Examples of Decisions include:

- The creative brief was approved

- We will wait until spring to reevaluate this project
- Josh will attend the conference
- We aren't moving forward with Company ABC's proposal

QUESTIONS

This section is my personal scratch pad for questions I have. These I will ask specific people about or perform my own research on after the meeting is over. My favorite acronym in business is GTS: *Google that shit*. If there's a word I don't understand, I make sure to write it down and look it up as soon as possible. Sometimes it can be embarrassing to ask something you don't know so jotting these things down ensures that you can get up to speed quickly.

Questions can also be the things you need to connect about with a smaller group that might not be appropriate for everyone in that meeting. These questions range from: "How will we support this initiative? What is the priority of this project? Who will I assign to work on this? Who do I know who can vet these vendors?" My questions help me have a place to keep a log of the things I need to understand or get to the bottom of. I typically don't send these out unless there is so much uncertainty between us and them that they have to figure out those items on their side as well. If it's something specific that someone needs to do and report back, those items get dropped down into Next Actions.

NEXT ACTIONS

This section is the blocking and tackling of who needs to do what and by when. I'm a stickler for getting the action item down, writing the person's initials on it, and establishing a due date before the end of the meeting. If time doesn't allow me to talk through all of the Next Actions, I will just assign a date and see if anyone pushes back on my aggressive timeline. Speed is key in all situations. The faster you move, the more you will get done.

Speaking of speed, I'm a believer that all notes should be ideally sent out the same day. If it's a late meeting, I'm good with having a 24-hour window but it shouldn't take a week to get notes out from a meeting. I set the tone with this in my team very early on so now it's an expectation. I don't do much note taking these days as I've trained our leaders and process/project team to duplicate my best practices. I recommend you do the same by first setting the standard and then expecting it from your team.

You are running a business. Your meeting notes belong in a consolidated place where all necessary parties have access – not just on a legal pad that only you can access. I use (you guessed it) a series of spreadsheets to hold all our meeting notes. Every meeting held in Cardone Venture's history – if I was present for it or not – is instantly searchable by date and type (executive, department-specific, all-team, etc.). It's been the same process from the start.

AFTER THE MEETING

I'm all about measuring the quantifiable benefits that everyone is taking out of meetings. The sum of a meeting's value is not what happens inside the meeting – it's what gets executed after it. This is where documentation that has occurred prior to and during the meeting becomes most useful. It all comes together to create a tool that you will use to hold everyone (including yourself) to what has been laid out in the meetings. Talk is cheap – and that's all meetings are. You can have the greatest and highest energy meetings in the world, but if your team doesn't take action after them, you will never scale your business.

Once the notes are sent out, I use them as my list of items I need to complete and I try to get them done within a day. As soon as my items are complete, I respond to the email with the notes letting the team know the completion status. I expect that they do the same – as their items get finished, they let the team know. This creates a high level of accountability and prevents you from showing up to the next meeting with unfinished items from the previous meeting. A couple of months ago, one of our business units was not hitting targets. The pace of the team felt lethargic and there was a lack of clarity as to the status of important initiatives and who was responsible. I started joining their weekly meetings and realized after 2 weeks that the process was being followed with the notes but the leaders were not executing on their Next Actions. Want to know how I fixed it? I showed up to the next meeting, reminded people of the value and the "why" behind it, and after the meeting, I sent my completion status within 5 hours. Lead by example.

If you value your time and don't want to see it being wasted in purposeless meetings, that will rub off on your team. There will be a time when they are the ones running the meetings (the goal is Duplication, after all), so part of teaching them to be successful in your absence is the art of running value-add meetings. One of the ways I drive this into our culture is by asking this at the end of our meetings: "Did we hit our target for this meeting?" As you grow further removed from the hands-on work of your business, the effectiveness of your meetings and their structure will be crucial to maintaining your awareness and input on what's going on at all levels of your organization.

Now it's much easier to implement a process like the one I've listed above when you're doing a handful of meetings a day with a small team, versus when your entire week is loaded with them and you have teams on teams on teams. So have these practices in place – before you get what you've been wishing for and you have too many conversations to have and not the right containers for them. It's time to open your calendar and create your containers. Start The Work.

YOUR TEAM

YOUR TEAM

We've invested time into you and your culture. Now, it's time to round things off by focusing on your team.

If you're saying you have this big Mission and Vision – but you don't have a mechanism to help get people aligned with all of it, things will never start clicking.

The rest of this book focuses on creating this alignment specifically with the team that you lead. Your team is different from your culture. The culture impacts everyone. But as you grow, only a handful of people in your culture will actually be on your team. We're going to work through spending time and creating activities in your schedule that pour into the specific individuals who report directly to you.

We're about to get into the nitty gritty, learn the distinct and unique goals of your team members, then position them to scale their careers and the business simultaneously. We may be diving into particulars, but we don't want to get lost in the weeds. As we dive into this final section, I want you to return to the well out of which everything flows: your Duplication Activity. That way, when you set up processes that invest time into your team, that valuable energy isn't going to waste. We're going to start the work of measuring performance through Metrics – which will allow you to monitor how things are going without having to micromanage every single person in your business.

To motivate and rally the team towards scaling, we're going to come up with structures and plans for incentives that gamify growth and reward your team for elevating what they bring to the table. If the business is scaling, but employees aren't getting anything for it, how long will that scaling last? You'll be dealing with constant turnover that is costly to the organization and disheartening to your high performers if they can't see how they win as the business grows.

Finally, we're going to check in on our team's goals. Just like you dream of scaling your business, they have personal, professional, and financial goals of their own. How can those become aligned with the path you want your business to tread? Those are answers that can come out in efficient, deep, and meaningful PPF conversations.

Investing time into your team is one of the greatest things you can do to scale your business. Done well, with calculated and efficient effort, your team will gladly support and share in your commitment to scaling with them. This means more talent knocking on your door looking to work with you and an organization where everyone believes in the Mission of growing and helping your customers just as much as you do.

All the exclusive resources I mention in the book are ready for you to use, along with videos, tools, and extras that I couldn't share in this book, go to StartTheWorkTools.com.

YOUR
TEAM

- ☑ **TEAM GOALS**
- ☐ METRICS
- ☐ INCENTIVES
- ☐ 1:1'S
- ☐ THE CYCLE OF SCALING

CHAPTER 15

TEAM GOALS

One of the most highly leverageable activities you can do inside your business is to get clear on your team member's goals. Their goals are the reason that they show up every day. Their goals are the fuel that can turn an average team member into a high-value leader who will fight for their goals (and those of the company). The only way to get someone to care about your goals is to care about theirs. Read that again. When you demonstrate that you care about your team member's individual goals, you can leverage both of your efforts and time.

Think about a traditional org chart. Let's say you have 5 team members working for you who you've never asked about their goals. They show up, clock in and out, and never go above and beyond. Yet here you are, proclaiming you want to grow your business, putting in extra hours because you recognize that the growth is going to require you to do more. The only reason you're putting the energy in is because you have goals and see how the extra time is going to increase your chances of achieving your goals.

This is very clear to a business owner, and it is likely why you're investing time into reading this book. But who takes the time to explain this to your team? When was the last time you sat your team members down and said, "You can achieve everything you want in life through hard work and determination. So what do you want to achieve? It's my job to help show you the path to get there". Very few leaders have this conversation and yet it's the single most impactful communication you can have with your team members. This is how we've grown from 0 to 220 employees in such a short amount of time. The growth comes from the existing team adding valuable skills to the business while they're actively being the best in their role. How do they do this?

Working more.

Why would someone willingly (and happily) work more? Because they believe and see that the work will get them where they want to go. They will show up early, stay late, work on weekends, and produce 2x to 3x of a team member in the same role. I've seen this happen time and time again because high performers want to be pushed. I know this because I'm one of them. This personal, professional, and financial goal process changed my life. During my summer internship when I was twenty years old, I reported to the VP of Administration, who took me under her wing and gave me insight into the different projects and opportunities within the organization. At the two-month mark of my employment, she asked me to start formulating my personal, professional, and financial goals for the next one, three, and five years. I remember sitting at my desk staring at a blank legal pad for hours. I had never put my goals into such concrete buckets. I had always thought of my goals as a wish list that felt far-off and idealistic; I, however, had an assignment and was determined to complete it so I could have my PPF conversation with her. Here is what I came up with:

Personal:

- Find supportive friends
- Eat one green thing every day

Professional:

- Be a manager and lead a team
- Travel monthly for work

Financial:

- Save $5K to put down and buy a nicer car (I desperately wanted to get rid of my 1993 Buick Century)
- Make $15 per hour

I felt silly writing these down. You know that feeling? You put down in writing what you really want, and it seems so unattainable compared to where you're currently at. At the time, I was in the middle of college, still financially dependent on my parents, and had no idea what I wanted to do with the economics courses I was taking. Despite feeling silly, I couldn't lie to myself.

This shortlist was exactly what I wanted, and I could close my eyes and imagine being a confident businesswoman leading teams and rolling around in a new car. This seemingly silly exercise transformed my life and was the starting point for the goal-oriented, make-it-happen person I am today. Because she tapped into my goals, I wanted to prove to myself and her that I would do whatever it takes. I bought courses, read books, and put in 20+ more hours than my peers because of the drive I had to get where I wanted to go. This came from the belief that the organization would reward me as I added more value to myself and that translated into more value to the organization.

Every team member should have the same opportunity I had: a leader who cared about my goals and pushed me to figure out what I really wanted so that she could help coach me to get there. This conversation took 45 minutes of her time and added hundreds of hours of productivity and output to the organization. We're going to dive into how to make this PPF process a staple in your organization.

PERSONAL, PROFESSIONAL, AND FINANCIAL GOALS

The personal, professional, and financial goal structure creates buckets to organize any goal a person can have. These three categories touch everything. After having over a thousand PPF conversations to date, I've yet to come across a goal that doesn't fall into one of these buckets.

PERSONAL GOALS

Personal goals encompass a wide variety of things that people can be motivated by from a personal standpoint: working out, playing the clarinet, traveling abroad, spending time with loved ones, learning a new language, becoming a great baker... They run the gamut. It will surprise you what some of your team members' personal goals are, and I can promise that you will learn something unexpected with every PPF conversation you have.

PROFESSIONAL GOALS

Professional goals are focused on areas of accomplishment. This can include learning new skills, learning new ways of operating, taking on new responsibilities, being promoted, starting new projects, receiving awards or recognition for those efforts, and attracting mentors into your life.

FINANCIAL GOALS

Financial goals should always be a target that is tied to a specific financial outcome. This could be your net worth, establishing passive income, having the ability to purchase gifts, paying off school loans, being able to afford family care services, target salary, paying off debt, etc.

By breaking down individual goals into these three categories, the actions required to accomplish these goals can be more focused and intentional. This helps create the overall plan and compartmentalize the goals in a structured format. For each section, you should have them define what success looks like in 1 year, 3 years, and 5 years. When you create a longer time horizon, it allows your team members to think about whom they could be and what they want to create in their lives. It fleshes out a roadmap for them of the milestones they will hit. Eventually, you will have them complete the Duplication Activity so that they can look at where they're spending their time and if it's in accordance with where they want to go. For now, let's stay focused and nail the PPF conversation as this is part of your Duplication Activity.

Why do you think we ask about personal goals in a work context? There's rarely pushback on the professional and financial, seeing as though both of those categories are tied to the work the team member does with you. But personal goals are just as important. The reality is that our team members are not robots. As nice as it would be to hire people who only want to work eighteen hours a day and who eat, breathe, and sleep our business, that's just not real life. People work to be able to fund and create an impactful personal life with the people they care about. Your team members want to buy a boat to hang out on the river during a hot summer day and be able to take their family on trips. Others are motivated by overcoming their fears by doing stand-up comedy once a month or running a marathon. So to the extent that you're just ignoring this whole side of your team members' lives, you're missing a big component of what's driving them. And as their coach, it's critical to know what truly drives and inspires them. That's your job.

Think for a moment about your own personal, professional, and financial goals. Even for the most career-driven people, when you look at their goals, the conquest is part of why chasing financial goals is so thrilling, but the ability to put yourself, your family, and the people you care about in a position to thrive personally is oftentimes the root of the true motivation. Your team is no different, which is why personal goals come first and often take the most time to establish.

YOUR GOALS

Before you go and set the expectation that your team members need to be goal-oriented and share them with you, I need to remind you that the culture of setting and sharing goals starts at the top. As the leader of the organization, whether you thought it was your responsibility until now or not, you need to make your goals clear to the team. This is essential to duplicate your efforts, through your example, to again determine what to Start, Continue, Delegate, and Stop as you see who is ready to fill in certain roles as part of their goals.

To the extent that you're not sharing your goals, you're missing one of the most transformational elements of any high-performing team. When you start talking about things that you're going after, it inspires the people in your environment. It reinforces that you're creating a high-performance team because you're a high performer. You should have so much confidence in where you're going because you're committed to doing the work every single day to push your goals forward.

Before we move on to the process for your team member's goals, I want you to go back to Chapter 1 and reflect on the personal, professional, and financial goals you wrote down. As you review them, identify which goals you're going to start sharing with your team. By no means do you need to share everything with them – only choose the goals that you are willing to share and start publicly going after them. When I say "share", I don't mean schedule a meeting with your entire team to walk through your goals. Find ways to publicly share which goals you're currently going after. If you want to complete a half marathon, start sharing on social media your training schedule and a countdown to race day. If one of your goals is to spend more time with your significant other, post a photo on Instagram of the two of you and share why date night is a priority. You should always be promoting these areas of growth that you're targeting. Grant Cardone shares his goals by wearing a shirt that says, "Billionaire in the Making".

While I've been writing this book, I've been sharing updates on how many words I've written and how many I have left to hit my target. This doesn't just promote my goals to our team; it also promotes them to clients, prospective clients, competitors, and candidates. There should be no confusion for anyone that your culture is goal-oriented, and that starts with you. The biggest goal that you should be promoting all the time is your Vision. Your Vision statement should be your ultimate professional goal. There shouldn't be a day that goes by where you don't talk about your Vision to someone.

GO ALL IN

You don't have to implement this process. Many businesses don't. Before you jump feet first into this PPF process, these are my three requirements:

DEEPLY CARE

You have to deeply care about your team members. If you have low regard for them and choose to believe that your success isn't integrally tied to their success, there's no need to roll this process out. This isn't just a tool to implement to pretend like you care or to try to fabricate a high-performing culture. Your team members will smell the insincerity a mile away. This only works when the leader is truly bought into the idea that they are in the people business and that their team's success matters.

COMMIT

Once you roll out this process, you need to commit to it. You cannot just have a PPF conversation with the people you like and not have it with others. Everyone who reports to you should have the same opportunity. This is an ongoing investment of your team into your team members.

FOLLOW THROUGH

Early in my career, one of the worst mistakes I made in the PPF process was having goal conversations with people and then never talking about them again. I failed in my role as a coach. You have to remember that goals are sensitive to most people because it's an acknowledgment of something they want but don't know how to get or have tried and failed in the past. A goal wouldn't be a goal if it was easy or if you had already done it. So there's already this hesitation your team members will have about sharing them. Once they do, you need to be responsible for following through. You don't get to sit back and watch them fail because if they're quitting on their goals, what makes you think they're going to continue to fight for yours?

THE PPF CONVERSATION

Ahead of the PPF conversation, you should provide the team member with a PPF Form. Use the version we used in Chapter 1 as your template (you can find it at

StartTheWorkTools.com). This does not need to be fancy, but it should list the categories and time frames. The best time to send this document is in the first couple of weeks during Onboarding. I share our tried-and-true onboarding process in my book *TeamWork* (steal shamelessly from it). When you share it early on, the team member will have a month to review it and start jotting down ideas ahead of the conversation. It's not a requirement that everyone fills out each category. Ideally, they do, but if they are struggling with a few of them, that's where you come in and guide the conversation. The form is merely a place for them to prep their ideas ahead of the conversation. When you introduce the form, don't be rigid. This process can be challenging for many team members because they've never gone through this before. You want to make them as comfortable as possible and ease their nerves.

The PPF conversation is not rocket science. It is literally as simple as sitting down with somebody and saying, "It's fantastic that you've joined our organization! I know you're two months in with us, and it's time for us to sit down and discuss your personal, professional, and financial goal planning because it's important to me and to this organization that you achieve your goals. As we grow, we want to align your goals with the business's goals so that we can win together. With that, let's get going! Walk me through your one-year personal goals". It's that simple.

Once you ask for their goals, write down what they're saying and make sure to be listening because it's going to be on you to ask great questions. You'll find that your team members will initially be vague. They might say that one of their one-year personal goals is to get in the best shape of their life. That's a great goal! But you need more context. This is where the SMART framework comes into play.

Here's the deal: it's likely that you suck at asking questions. It's not necessarily your fault. There wasn't training in school as to how to be a great question-asker, but that has to change. When using the SMART framework, you'll be able to run through what questions to ask to get clarity quickly.

Here's what **SMART** stands for:

Specific. "What exactly are you going to accomplish?"

Measurable. "How can you track the progress?"

Attainable. "Are you able to accomplish this goal?"

Relevant. "Why is this important to you?"

Timely. "When will you accomplish this goal?"

Let's say a team member shared the "get in the best shape of my life" goal with me, here are some questions I would ask before moving on to the next goal: What activities are you going to do to get in shape (running, weights, yoga, etc.)? What's the best shape you've ever been in? How long ago was that? Why aren't you in that shape any longer? How often will you need to work out? Do you need to change your diet as well?

Depending on the answers, I would ask additional questions to ensure that I fully understand this goal. After I do, I'd move on to ask about the three-year goal and then start the question-asking process all over again. After we've gone through all nine of the goals (one-, three-, and five-year goals for each PPF category), I ask the team member to send me their updated goals within the next twenty-four hours.

Because people set goals in a variety of ways, I do provide a worksheet with the SMART framework because it's helpful to some people. I personally don't like to get that granular when setting my own goals, but many of my clients and team members thrive using that structure because it allows them to further break down their goals.

When you're using the SMART framework in the conversation, don't literally ask, "How can we make that more specific?" or "Is that relevant to you?" You need to train yourself how to be naturally curious while knowing that the outcome is for you to help this person achieve these goals. The point of the conversation is to connect, not perfectly dial in every detail. You need the most important pieces. If your team member wants to have a weekly date night with their husband, you better ask what the husband's name is and be genuinely curious.

Once the conversation has taken place, it's the team member's responsibility to send their goals to you, ideally in the updated SMART format. The team member should then add these goals to their weekly one-on-ones to give you their updates on where they are making progress and where they are stalling. I dive deep into the one-on-one process in the next chapter. In an ideal scenario, Incentive Plans are established after the PPF conversation so that the team member can understand what they need to do to earn more money through selling your products and/or driving operational efficiencies. Incentive Plans are always the trickiest part. It can be hard to craft them outside of sales. But we can do hard things, right?

When it comes to the Incentive Plan, the goal is for every single team member in your organization to have full clarity on exactly what they need to do that day to make more money. The PPF conversation is the starting point for creating this Incentive Plan. Without clarity on their financial goals, it's hard to create targets for what activities they need to do that day to accomplish your goals. On the business side, if you're not closing your books and reviewing your financials on a monthly basis, you will avoid creating non-sales incentive plans because you won't have confidence in the impact that the activity is having on the financials. Only lazy business owners don't review their financial statements monthly. Don't be lazy! Get this discipline in.

REMEMBER YOUR ROLE

I can't tell you how many times I messed these conversations up, and it's taken me years to feel confident. I can assure you that your first few conversations will feel awkward and you will run into some hiccups. That's normal. Just keep pushing through and stay focused on why you're doing this: you're connecting with your team members and trying to understand what motivates them. If you keep that intention at the core of this process, the minutia doesn't matter.

Developing the process of learning about your team, their goals, and what they want to accomplish should give you an even deeper sense of purpose when it comes to your goals. Now you begin to elevate your influence as a leader because your goals are so big that your leaders can see achieving their goals alongside yours. This is one of the most important and exciting parts of learning what to Stop, Continue, Delegate, and Start: the outcomes you choose create a ripple effect on helping you and your team achieve their goals. See, this isn't just about how you spend your time to help you accomplish more. It's about how to start the work of helping your team members achieve success on your way to building and scaling yourself and your business. This is the ultimate win-win-win situation for your people, for you, and for your organization. It transforms people to be, do, and have more than they thought possible. They will have found a place that supports them, which is one of the rarest experiences you get to create for your team.

Do not take your team's goals lightly – and definitely don't sleep on mastering the process of communicating with them. If you haven't done so already, add the PPF conversations for each of your team members who report to you to your Duplication Activity as a Start. It's that time: Start The Work.

YOUR
TEAM

- ☑ TEAM GOALS
- ☑ **METRICS**
- ☐ INCENTIVES
- ☐ 1:1'S
- ☐ THE CYCLE OF SCALING

CHAPTER 16

METRICS

If you are serious about your business, you will create Metrics for every role. Metrics are the central nervous system for your organization – letting you know what's working, what you should duplicate, and what's broken that needs to be fixed. The challenge you likely face is that you drive the business. You have a certain way that you do things that makes everything work. This ultimately is a recipe for having a job for the rest of your life. If we want to scale your business, these qualitative factors are going to have to become measurable, quantitative Metrics.

As you duplicate yourself and move further into your role as the leader of your organization, Metrics will become one of the most valuable tools that you have. One of the first markers of someone who is working on, not inside, their business is their ability to set measurable standards for each of their team members. Having hard data that you can use to quantify the performance of team members and their departments will expedite your ability to scale. If you notice revenue is stagnant or declining, that hard data will take out the guesswork about why that is happening.

If revenue is in fact going up, but not as fast as you want it to be, Metrics will also indicate which levers need to be pulled.

On the topic of duplication – which is essential to scaling businesses – Metrics make positions far easier to replicate. You don't want your clients and customers to be in love with a particular person on your team, you want them to be in love with the process and end result that your business creates. Taking the brightest members of your team and putting the qualities that make them great into measurable, quantifiable data will help you train new people with the same standard of excellence. This chapter will teach you how to take the qualitative factors that make your business work and turn them into operating Metrics that you can track with ease.

KPI'S VS METRICS

It's funny to me that all things lead back to your goals as a business owner. Even Metrics? Yes. You creating Metrics for your coordinator is directly tied to your goals.

How? Let's take a look at this:

KPI VS METRICS

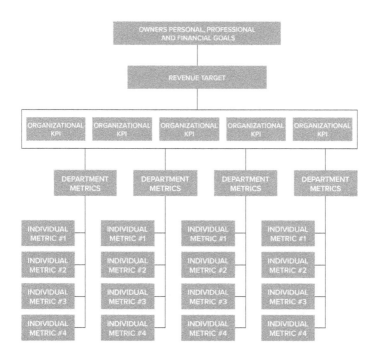

1. **Owner's Personal, Professional, and Financial Goals:** Your goals are the driving force behind your business and should be cultivated and protected at all costs. When you believe in your goals, you will have an unwavering commitment to the success of your organization at the granular level. You'll realize that everything inside your business is a representation of you. When you take your goals seriously, you take the Metrics in your business seriously because they are the only thing that actually gets you to your target.

2. **Revenue Target:** The revenue target creates the ultimate clarity on where your organization is going. This is where the Revenue Algorithm from the Annual Planning chapter comes into play. Once you've used the Revenue Algorithm, you will have the overarching target for the financial goal of the business. But you can't possibly have confidence and clarity in hitting this very specific number unless you are clear on the most important levers to generate revenue inside your business – enter KPIs.

3. **Organizational KPIs:** Key Performance Indicators are the critical Metrics that are used to evaluate and track the performance of a specific outcome of an organization, process, or activity. The purpose of a KPI is to provide clarity on whether or not the organization is on track to hit its goals and objectives. You use them to identify

what's working and what's broken so that you know where to spend your time. They are the most important Metrics in your business. All Organizational KPIs are directly tied to revenue generation. If we're on track with our KPIs, we will hit the revenue that's tied out to each of them. I suggest you structure your organization's KPIs similarly. There are lots of smaller measurements that drive the results of KPIs – these are known as Metrics. All KPIs are Metrics but not all Metrics are KPIs – reread that. Now let's dive into why.

4. **Metrics (Department/Individual):** Metrics are quantifiable measures that businesses use to evaluate and track various aspects of their operations and performance. They provide a way to objectively assess different aspects of the business, such as sales, revenue, customer satisfaction, and employee productivity. Metrics can be used to monitor progress towards business goals and objectives, identify areas for improvement, drive decision-making, evaluate the performance of individual departments, teams, or employees, measure the impact of new initiatives or projects, and facilitate communication between different departments and stakeholders. The specific Metrics a business uses will depend on its goals, objectives, industry, and operations. It's important to choose the right Metrics to track, as they will provide valuable information to help drive business success.

Metrics should be relevant, actionable, and measurable, and should provide meaningful insights into the performance of the business. I will note that sometimes, it's easier for our clients to identify KPIs after they've listed the Metrics they track. The most important, revenue-driving Metrics are the best starting point for you to choose your KPIs.

Until you start tracking output by role in your business, it's almost impossible to set real targets. If you're like Sean Stagnates and don't measure much currently, don't worry. You can still make a change today in your business by setting targets for individual team members, products/services, and department output. I'm a big believer in progress over perfection on rolling out targets. You don't have to have everything perfect to make progress on the most important things immediately. But ensure that you also roll out a mechanism for tracking so that you can assess the progress. This can be as simple as a tracker to measure output. Don't overcomplicate the process.

GOOD TEAM MEMBERS LOVE METRICS

Every employee under me has clearly defined Metrics that I use to analyze their performance. At the end of each week, each team member who reports to me sends me this data for review. In our current growth cycle of Cardone Ventures, I only have Department Heads reporting to me – which means that they have team members reporting to them. This report from each department head has the Department Metrics, which is an aggregation of the most important output of their department as it's now the job of the leader to drive the individual Metrics that make up the successes or failures of the department. The Department Heads have their team members report their individual Metrics to them which allows them to give me an accurate understanding of what's really happening. The important thing that you can't miss in this equation is that, at one point, the department head was once the team member who was in the role driving specific Metrics. That's how small businesses grow into big businesses – team members duplicate themselves and grow into leadership roles. So even if you don't have department heads now, the team members who are currently doing the work should be the future leaders if they are great at their role. But how would you know they're great if you never measured them?

People outside our business often ask me what I did to get people to be collaborative in a reporting process like this – which sometimes involves reporting that this week did not go so well. What I've discovered is a simple truth: if someone is not willing to have their performance measured, they are not worth having on your team. Imagine if Steph Curry didn't want to know his three-point percentage, or if Randy Moss plugged his ears when people talked about how many receiving yards he had in a particular game.

Ignorance is not bliss. If you have a team who wants to grow along with your scaling business, Metrics won't just be a tool for your sake – they will be a springboard for them to reach their goals faster as well. There's no hiding in a business that's scaling. In contrast, a stagnant business is one that creates shadows for people to coast in. Metrics are the light that reveals all.

When I was an intern, there were no Metrics for me. This is probably a good thing, considering I was an intern stuffing binders and the business had a bunch of other priorities above giving the intern targets to meet. But, being the competitive person I am, I took my Metrics into my own hands. My job was to stuff binders in preparation for this big event they were putting together in Las Vegas. This was back when everything was printed into these boxes and had to be manually sorted and bound afterwards. I started marking how fast I was putting each binder together and measured my productivity over the entire course of my two-month internship. I don't think anyone ever reviewed my Metrics, but creating them made me better and more motivated at my job. Your team, if they give a shit about the work they do, want Metrics. Give them Metrics and review them regularly.

But here's the thing: even if they don't want them, you still need to have them. This isn't a negotiation or up for debate. It needs to be the new standard in your business that everyone has Metrics that they're reporting on – ideally daily. The measurement and refinement of daily activity is the source of everything you need to know in order to grow. In the same way that you now have a heightened awareness of where you're spending your time, you should have this same outlook as it relates to team members. Where the heck are they spending their time? The more you focus on this initially, the easier and less resistance you will find as you grow.

I recently became operationally responsible for a business that we bought and the first thing I did was roll out a daily production tracker to all production roles. It was met with agreement from many but significant pushback from others. This did not make me popular. I got every objection about why this was inefficient, took too long to do every day, and wasn't feasible. Blah blah blah. At the end of the day, I wasn't asking. It was an expectation. It's okay to put your foot down in your business and make Metrics and tracking mandatory, even when it upsets people. I find that the people who push back the hardest are the ones who don't want to be held accountable. When you come to terms with this, you get to make a decision: are you going to let their lack of accountability get in the way of you hitting your goals? For me, that answer is a strong "no."

WHERE TO START WITH METRICS

Now you might be asking, "Where do I start with setting up Metrics?" The challenge is that Metrics are not always obvious. Setting these up for revenue generators, such as salespeople, is easy. If you're creating Metrics for a role that you used to do yourself, that should be easy. You know what's possible and what reasonable expectations are. I do find that many business owners can struggle with separating what makes them unique vs what their numerical contribution was when they were in the role. If you struggle with this in your own role, I suggest you pull up your calendar from the days when you were in the role and look at your output. How many meetings did you host? How many did you close? How long did each installation take? How many times did you follow up? How many resumes did you review? This should help you start to map out the important Metrics in your role.

When it comes to non-revenue generating roles like account managers, accountants, and legal, laying out the statistics of success is much more nuanced. The magic formula will be unique to your business, what challenges your team has to overcome, and what your goals are as a leader.

Because of all this, setting up Metrics will begin as one big experiment that starts with your team member's job description and time allocation. Look at where they're spending their time I recommend you have all of your team members complete the Duplication Activity and then derive the quantifiable Metrics that their role should be responsible for based on this breakdown. When clients come to us to help them 10X their business, they often say that the reason they haven't set up Metrics is because they're waiting for somebody to tell them which ones to implement. In the downloadable available at *StartTheWorkTools.com*, I've listed my top Metrics across the most important roles in any organization and encourage you to use them as a starting point but you have to learn how to establish these on your own as well in order to keep growing.

Expecting someone else to figure this out for you creates laziness inside your organization. Look at where your team member is spending their time. How do you measure those activities? Now you have a Metric! You aren't struggling with Metrics because you're not smart enough to figure them out – it's likely because you've never really looked at the work of each role with a quantifiable lens. All it takes is a commitment to establishing them, tracking them, and editing them as results come in. What's worse: having the wrong Metrics or not setting them at all? If you go with the former – you've started the process of discovering the right Metrics. My rule of thumb is each team member has 10-15 Metrics, each department has 15-20, and the organization has 8-10 KPIs.

The intention isn't to measure everything – it's artfully assessing what are the most important contributions this role/department makes to the organization. You could easily list hundreds of Metrics that a single role could be measured by. This is not the intention. You are not trying to make a list of everything this role does. You are strategically looking at each role's most important contribution to the growth of the department and organization and limiting this number to 10-15.

I have a team member who's established a $2 million arm of our business. He started out in an internal finance function and moved into building out a client facing department that now generates revenue. This is a major transition, driven by personal initiative. While we're all about the calculated approach at Cardone Ventures, our top performers know that there's an element of experimentation that comes with trailblazing. This team member came to me the other day for a check in. He was frustrated, explaining that he'd been so focused on revenue generating Metrics for this new service that he didn't consider the quality of the work that his team was producing. These missing metrics are key to the client facing work that he and his new department is doing – and he was realizing that he hadn't been property incentivizing his team.

I see realizations like these as wins. Take this story as a kick in the butt. Your Metrics don't have to be perfect. They just have to be decided and constantly reviewed. Don't get tripped up over what you don't know. Pick a starting point and iterate. You might forget to measure something that's vital to the success of a role. When you find that out, it's as simple as fixing it! It can also be helpful to leverage Metrics from other businesses in your industry. What Metrics are they using? What are the key drivers that they value in assessing the productivity of their employees? Copy others and test their methods out, but make sure you're looking at them using the context of your business.

Something many of our business owners struggle with is the trackability of Metrics. They'll get all excited about having designed "the perfect Metrics" for X position or Y department, only to discover a week or so in that tracking those Metrics is logistically impractical or inefficient. When this happens, we remind them that the best Metrics are the ones you can and will track. Don't get discouraged if this happens to you. This is part of the iterative process. As long as you keep this as a focus that you're constantly assessing and revising, I assure you that you will create the right structure for your team members, departments, and organization. In moments that you find yourself being discouraged because it's not working the way you wanted it to, I find it helpful to think of myself as playing a game. You might have thrown an interception, but one bad play doesn't mean you've lost. Just keep playing. Know that the work you're putting in will lead you to winning. The only way you lose is by giving up. So don't give up – iterate and keep going. You've got this.

METRICS VS INCENTIVE METRICS

For you to keep this iterative mentality in place with the Metrics for your team members, you need to create a mechanism for you to review their Metrics regularly. The mechanism I use is the One-on-Ones. I have with each of my team members every other week. I'll discuss this in detail in the following chapter but it's important to note here as it might feel like you have all of these new numbers to review without structure. Have no fear – the One-on-Ones is your new best friend. There is a specific section dedicated to Metrics in the One-on-Ones form that I propose you use. What you'll notice is it's a placeholder for your team member to update you on where they're at with their Metrics. This will be an important conversation for them because there are a handful of their Metrics that should be categorized as Incentive Metrics where you establish targets – meaning they get paid more when they hit an established target for the Metric that's above and beyond what's expected in the role.

You need to be careful about the targets you set for Incentive Metrics as you will find out quickly that people will work their pay plans. This is a beautiful and dangerous thing. Let's say you have a Marketing Manager who you have tasked with driving new patients into your practice. You currently get 100 leads per month and you decide that you will give the Marketing Manager an extra 5% of her base salary if she can get 300 leads per month. Great idea – wrong execution. What if she drives in 300 new patients off a free cleaning ad? If your practice specializes in aesthetic dentistry, you are looking for a specific type of patient who isn't likely coming into your practice off of a free cleaning promotion. It was the wrong Incentive Metric target. Here's where people get confused: the Metric of the number of leads per month is important and should be raised but that's not the Metric that you pay more for someone to hit. It's simply a Metric that their role is responsible for growing. A better way to incentivize would be to give a percentage of production above what you're currently producing based on the traffic that's brought in from the Marketing Manager. You're not paying on the new leads per month – you're paying for what drives the business, which is revenue.

So once you have your Metrics in place, the fun begins. This is where you start to see the biggest shift in your business because you'll be able to try new things and measure their effectiveness. You're not just measuring things and assuming they're fixed – the idea is they improve because you're paying attention to what impacts them. To prepare for your one-on-ones where your team members are sharing with you where they're at with their Metrics.

BELOW TARGET

When somebody is failing to hit a target, the first thing you need to ask them is "what are you running into?" Getting context is important but it's critical that the conversation stays centered on what needs to happen to get back on track.

Sometimes there are external factors at play when someone's work is slipping. You might find out there's a personal issue at play – and the current lapse in performance is going to make sense. The important thing is to not assume why the person didn't hit the target simply because they weren't able to. Transparency is one of our core values at Cardone Ventures – which makes these conversations all the smoother. I strongly suggest you make this one of your values, too. When I know my team is being transparent with me, my ability (and willingness) to invest in the resources and support they need to succeed is higher. If I'm going to coach someone who's struggling to hit their Metrics, I'm not going to be effective if I don't know what's really going on. So by valuing transparency and inviting my team to present their Metrics to me in the good faith we all want to succeed, we are actually able to identify the issues to still hit the target.

Having Metrics and measuring performance allows you to nip problems in the bud. If someone starts to slip – for any reason – the numbers catch it and we are able to address the underlying issues. If you're looking at the overall numbers of your business and they show that performance has been leaking, the leakage is always a person. Just remember this. It always comes down to finding who is responsible and figuring out the issue. Are they unclear on the target? Are they fully trained on the function? Have they roleplayed the situation? This is what you need to identify to plug the holes. Until you get good at conversations like these, your business will struggle to meaningfully scale.

Feedback like this shouldn't be scary or unusual in your organization. Team members should get accustomed to knowing that they're there to problem solve. With our culture, we're at a point where people who miss Metrics are taking the initiative to come into my office, explain what they ran into, and share what the 3 possible solutions could be for getting it fixed. This level of transparency exists because we demand it and are pragmatic when issues arise. As a leader, you can't fly off the handle at your team when issues occur. Be direct and definitive. There's no room for emotion. Handle it and move to the next priority.

HITTING TARGETS

Winners win. High performers perform. The people who are consistently hitting and exceeding targets should be rewarded, celebrated, and promoted. They should know that you value them and that they are demonstrating true leadership through their results. High performers need this – especially if they're surrounded by people who are okay with "good enough." If your current culture is average at best, it can be demoralizing to the handful of high performers on your team that you need to help you grow your business. Exceeding a target once is awesome but it's the consistency in the effort and result that you're looking for. Don't make the mistake of parading the results of your top performers who set a new benchmark one month just for them to plummet the next. I see this time and again with sales teams. Consistent results is the name of the target game. Once someone has demonstrated that they can replicate their results over and over again, their next opportunity is to move from a ME leader to a WE leader and coach their team members to be just as good, if not better than they are. That is the real art of scaling a business.

Working backwards, the end goal is to scale successfully. To scale successfully you need to know how to approach your time, yourself, your culture and your team so that you can strategically duplicate the outcomes you achieve. Putting in the work to establish, track, and update Metrics across your team will set the example for how they measure their team. This is one of the least exciting things to do and constantly look at but it is what will drive real results and allow you to prioritize your time based on data rather than option. The business owners who prioritize creating Metrics for their team and establishing Incentive Metric targets are well on their way to creating a scalable business.

YOUR
TEAM

- ☑ TEAM GOALS
- ☑ METRICS
- ☑ **INCENTIVES**
- ☐ 1:1'S
- ☐ THE CYCLE OF SCALING

CHAPTER 17

INCENTIVES

You are reading this because you have an incentive to do so.

Learning new strategies and tools for running your organization isn't a requirement. In fact, most don't. You likely do it with the intention of acquiring new skills that will benefit you. You wouldn't be reading these words if there wasn't a bonus it could unlock. If I marketed this book by saying "spend 6 hours reading this and learn nothing" you hopefully wouldn't have even picked it up. You clearly have an incentive to learn this material. And yet, so many of us as business leaders expect our employees to do things without clearly outlined rewards to motivate them.

Think about the top performing member of your team who continues to show up to work early. They're hustling their butt off to have a quick turnaround – what's their reward? If that employee's workload is increasing because of their capacity to do more, but they aren't taking home more pay each month, you're in trouble once they do that math themselves. They have to see what's in it for them to sustain this type of performance. What is their growth plan?

Many business owners brag about having team members with them for years and years. At first glance, you could say that this demonstrates that the owner is a great leader. However, if the business hasn't grown and those team members aren't making more money today than when they started, I would argue that those are the wrong team members. They're okay coasting and doing what they have to do to get by. If you aren't incentivizing growth for your team, you're allowing stagnation. Unfortunately, this won't work if you're looking to substantially increase your revenue because in order for your business to grow, you and your team need to grow.

If you don't spend the time to figure out this incentives game, you will always feel the burden of the growth of your organization. As we discussed in Chapter 15, when you are the only person in your organization who has goals, who does it fall on for the business to grow? You! But when you have team members who also have goals and see how they can win with you, the work gets divided across your team. They start to push the boundaries and hit targets that exceed expectations. When this is your culture, your team members fight to win in their roles everyday which creates the opportunity for you to set expectations on the specific activities that they can take in order for them to make more money in your organization.

A REASON TO SCALE

Real scaling happens when every single member of your organization knows exactly the tasks, processes, and results it's going to take for them to make more money themselves. The vision for your scaled business doesn't just need to be large, every employee needs to be able to see themselves in it. It's not enough to set clear expectations for what you're looking for. These need to be backed up with incentives that leverage the goals of others into a force that can aid yours. I've discussed this concept previously in *TeamWork*, through the Employee Engagement Cycle. In a nutshell, the cycle ensures that each of your team members has a clear path from Alignment (onboarding/training), through Development (becoming the top performers at their level), and finally through to Transition (promotion).

EMPLOYEE ENGAGEMENT CYCLE

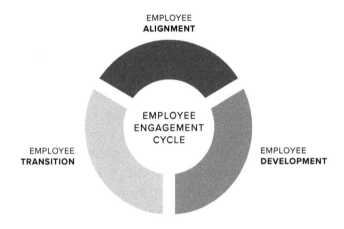

EMPLOYEE
ALIGNMENT

EMPLOYEE
ENGAGEMENT
CYCLE

EMPLOYEE
TRANSITION

EMPLOYEE
DEVELOPMENT

For those who read *TeamWork* and have implemented the Employee Engagement Cycle into your company culture, think of Incentives as added rewards during the Development phase which keep your team engaged in the day-to-day as they pursue the greater vision to Transition into more significant and higher paying roles. If your business is to do more, your team will have to do more. The more you grow and duplicate yourself, the less you can be around to micromanage that every process is being done correctly. If your business grows and somebody in it sees that their paycheck is staying the same – how invested would they be in continuing to help it scale? How invested would you be if you were in their shoes?

GAMIFYING

As the leader of a scaling business, your goal is to be gamifying the processes that are going to lead to growth. If you open up your monthly payroll and you see that people's incomes are going up, but your business' revenue is stagnant, you have placed your Incentives in the wrong spot but it's better to do this and then fix it, than have no Incentive Metrics at all. I like to tell our business owners that in the scheme of their 10-Year Revenue Target, they do not have a 10% of payroll problem. What I mean by this is, if you overpaid your team by 10% of your current payroll, while in pursuit of Metrics, that's not a problem. If you want a $30m business and you're currently at $3m with payroll being $300k, if you overpaid your current team by 10% each, that's $30k. You do not have a $30k problem! Your real problem is you don't have a $30m business. So get comfortable with the idea of potentially overpaying your team for a few months while you figure out the correct Metrics. The commitment I'm asking you to make is for every person in your organization to have a clear Incentive Plan based on Metrics of their role as we discussed in the last chapter.

One of my favorite 10X principles is this: Attention Follows Money. If you've signed a lease for your apartment, you're going to show up each night to live in your apartment. I go to the gym every day because I've invested money into a personal trainer. You get the idea. Where you go and what you do is directly tied to your money being there. This is why it's genius to have a cancellation fee at a high end restaurant. Their revenue for any given evening is based on how many tables are full and how quickly they're turning the tables for new patrons. If they have 30% last minute cancellations, there isn't anything they can do to fill those spots. Insert the cancellation fee and you're forcing a commitment on the dinner. As a customer, when you make the reservation, you're now more likely to show up because your money is tied to the commitment and it's likely that the restaurant's last minute cancellations decrease. Hence: Attention Follows Money.

So if you know this, how can you use this principle to your advantage? Gamifying the growth of your business means putting money where you need your team's attention to be. The first person that you have to do that for is yourself. As the business owner, you have to see the reward of putting your time and money into creating Incentive Plans for your team.

RULE OF INCENTIVES

My first, and most important, rule of Incentive Plans is everyone in your organization needs to have them. When I say everyone, I mean everyone. Not just your sales team. All employees should have an Incentive Plan laid out for them and this is how I make this easy:

1. Base Salary

2. Incentive Opportunity

3. Commission Opportunity

The base salary is fairly straightforward. This is the amount you pay someone for fulfilling the stated expectations of their role inside your organization. Think of this as what they get paid to complete the objectives listed in their job description.

The Incentive Opportunity should always be at least 10% of the person's base salary. Remember: you don't have a 10% payroll problem. You have an employee disengagement problem. When I'm determining the pay for a given role, I'd ideally like to make the base as close to market as possible while the Incentive is as high as possible. The higher the Incentive, the more opportunity you have to ensure the team member is focused on the right things that drive value. The Incentive should be established when you send the candidate the job offer – not something that gets added after the fact. When someone doesn't want to trade a lower base salary with higher total compensation for a smaller base and higher Incentive Opportunity, this tells me that the candidate is not truly confident in the results that they can deliver. Many of our Executives have a lower base than team members they lead but have a % of department growth as their Incentive so their total compensation is greater based on the value they contribute.

If you're posting for a role that you have duplicated many times and are already clear on the Incentive Metrics targets, you should share the specific Incentive Metric targets with the candidate. There's no need to surprise people with expectations after they've signed the offer when you knew that your expectations were high all along. I'd rather have a candidate choose to not move forward with us because they're scared off by the target than go through the process of hiring them, onboarding them, and having them quit because they weren't interested in doing the work associated with the role. If you don't have clarity on the specific targets ahead of hiring the role, I suggest you leave the Metrics undefined. This gives you the ability to work with the team member to figure out their Metrics vs Incentive Metrics within the first 4 weeks of their onboarding.

For the Commission Opportunity, in an ideal scene, this number should be infinite. I am a firm believer that every role should have the opportunity to sell inside your organization. This shouldn't be reserved for just your sales people. When you set up your organization like this, you are creating the opportunity for everyone to make 6 figures even if their base salary is half that. It attaches your team to your #1 problem: revenue. Now there are some business models that can't do this due to licensing restrictions. Examples such as medical practices and law firms are among the few that prevent this type of opportunity to exist. But if your industry doesn't have this limitation, you should implement this immediately and educate your team on it. Nothing makes me happier than when I see a recruiter or a videographer getting a $5500 payout because she sold Cardone Ventures products. It demonstrates that she cares about the thing that I care about – acquiring customers.

*In the downloadable at **StartTheWorkTools.com**, you'll find a template Incentive Plan that you can use with your team members. This is the exact template we use at Cardone Ventures. You're welcome.*

INCENTIVE METRIC TARGET CREATION

Now that you have the structure down, it's time to figure out how to create Incentive Targets for non-revenue generating roles. As I mentioned before, the place to start when determining the Incentive Metric targets is the role's Metrics. This is because you've already established how to measure this role. As you assess each Metric, you should determine what is the baseline for each Metric vs what you would be willing to pay more for because it's a more significant expectation. Here are some example Metrics vs Incentive Metrics:

Accounting

Metric: Closing the books by the 10th of the month.

Incentive: Closing the books by the 8th of the month with less than 2 errors.

Payroll Specialist

Metric: Submit payroll by the 3rd of the month.

Incentive: Submit payroll by the 3rd with 100% accuracy.

Recruiter

Metric: Close 10 roles per month.

Incentive: Close 12 roles on or before target start date.

Videographer

Metric: Submit 8 videos by EOW.

Incentive: Less than 2 production revisions needed for 10 videos.

Account Manager

Metric: Onboard 25 new clients in a timely manner.

Incentive: Onboard 30 new clients within 30 days with completed onboarding checklist.

Customer Service Representative

Metric: Resolve 80% of client inquiries in Customer Service Inbox within 48 hours.
Incentive: Resolve 95% of client inquiries in Customer Service Inbox within 24 hours.

You'll notice that I run these Metrics through a set of filters in order to create the Incentive Metric. The first filter is Timeliness. There are some activities that are so critical to the organization that I'm willing to pay extra for the team member to prioritize speed. Take the instance of closing our books. The baseline is on the 10th of every month. But if I can get this data and start making decisions on the 8th of the month, it will certainly stretch the team, but I'd be willing to pay more in order to make this happen.

When you use the timeliness filter, I strongly recommend that you also place an incentive for the same Metric on Accuracy. You don't just want your financial statements quickly – you want them done correctly. This is where Accuracy can be added as an Incentive for the Metric. I'd say they should have less than 2 errors.

The third filter I use is quantity. This is the most straightforward. You should pay money to have certain Metrics be higher than the baseline. For instance, if the Baseline Metric for an Account Manager is 50 clients but they're willing to take on 67, I would pay more for this additional quantity. You do have to be careful with this and use quantity sparingly when it comes to non-sales incentives. More is not always better. I wouldn't incentivize the same Account Manager who should be completing 25 calls per day to make 50 calls unless I was tracking the results of the calls. The result, in this case, should be the Incentive Metric or else you've accidentally paid more for effort that doesn't move the business forward.

Satisfaction is the 4th filter. This can be client or internal satisfaction depending on what the role does. If an Account Manager is supposed to have 50 clients but takes on 67, you have to ensure that quality work is still being completed. This is where a satisfaction Incentive is helpful because you can come up with a creative way to ensure your clients are receiving remarkable service. When it comes to internal roles, as your organization grows, you will hire team members whose job is to support the internal operations. In this situation, you can survey the departments that they serve to ensure that they are responsive.

My fifth, and most important filter: Process Incentive Metrics. These are less common, which makes them highly effective when you can implement them into your organization. This is where you artfully create an Incentive for someone to follow a process. I know what you're thinking. Why would you pay someone more for the job they're already supposed to be doing?

Well I never said that all incentives have to equal monetary gain. Tasks such as updating the CRM, following up with clients within 1 business day, and filing documents in the correct place are vital to scaling your business and yet most business owners don't see a way to get their team members to do these tasks.

Let's say that you have a free-wheeling sales rep who likes to fly by the seat of their pants. They may have great production numbers this month – which is yielding them the biggest commission checks that they've ever seen in their lives – but their job is about so much more than the moments when they close a deal. In order for their success to be sustainable, they have to maintain the processes that continue to set them and the company up for success such as updating the CRM and sending the contract to your Accounting department for processing. But if these crucial tasks are undervalued in comparison to the incentivized outcome, they're bound to get sloppy.

So you create an Incentive Metric for them to do these things. In this case, the Incentive Metric would be that they only get paid their full commission check if they pass a random audit of their CRM contacts to ensure they're updating their client notes. Let me tell you – you dock 25% off of a sales person's check once because they didn't follow the CRM process and you'll never have to have the conversation again. They will fall right in line with the process.

I have a rule. Whenever I get frustrated that a team member isn't doing something I want them to, instead of getting angry, I create a new Incentive and process. We spent $200k in ads a few months ago and I needed to get some client data out of our CRM just to find out that the sales team wasn't properly using it. I was furious. Here we had just invested hundreds of thousands of dollars into new leads and our sales team was treating them like their own personal list of contacts. We drafted the new policy with the random audits, rolled it out, and docked people's pay when they didn't abide by it.

They weren't happy but guess what? Neither was I. The following month, you better believe that the CRM was updated by each salesperson in accordance with our process. Coincidentally, we had the best month in the history of the company. Now, I'm not suggesting that we had our best month because our sales team utilized our CRM – that would be ridiculous. But I sure did sleep well that month knowing that the investments we were making in expanding our brand wasn't being treated with sloppy and disorganized follow up. Lesson to be learned: you just have to be creative on how you're engineering these Incentive Metrics.

INCENTIVE REVIEW

Now let's dive into how to review and adjust all of the Incentive Plans in your company. If you look at how your employee's pay is changing on a month to month basis, how is it lining up with your monthly revenue? Is success on the individual level indicative of your organization's growth? If you're answering no, you have the wrong incentives in place.

The reality is that the data is stupidly easy to interpret when you simply look at it. But most business owners run their organizations with no cadence for them to actually view their Incentive compensation. I do something simple at the end of every month so that I keep a pulse on this at the organizational level. I'll note that this is important as you'll start having leaders who are responsible for the Incentive Plans of their team members do this as well. They should know how you look at these things so I highly recommend that you give them a copy of this book so they can catch up to speed quickly.

Each month, our Controller prepares a spreadsheet that lists everyone's names and what they made the previous months. If their compensation went up, their name is in green, if it stayed the same, their name is in black, and if it went down, their names are in red. This gives me an easy way to see what's happening. If everyone is in the green but our revenue didn't grow last month, we have a problem. Similarly, if our revenue grows but we have very few greens, I need to dig deeper into why more team members aren't directly benefiting from the growth. For the team members in red, I'm always assessing why their income is going down. This is cause for concern and something you need to continue to pay attention to the following month. This might indicate early signs of disengagement. It also could demonstrate that you have the wrong Incentive Metrics.

Whatever the situation, it's time to do a little investigation into what's happening so that you can resolve it quickly. I'm a firm believer that if you pay attention to how much money your team is making, they'll pay attention to the organization's problems. You can't forget that the reason they show up every day is for a paycheck. Sure – they might like you, your clients, or their work bestie. But at the end of the day, if you stopped paying them entirely, they wouldn't continue to show up. The nature of the relationship is financial. So if you are paying attention to how they can make more money by creating more value, you're solving a problem that helps you scale. Make it a goal to create millionaire employees. What would that look like in your business? How could you make that possible? Focus your high performers on big targets like this and I guarantee you will create the engagement that you've been missing in your business.

INCENTIVES UNLEASH GROWTH

If you're serious about scaling your business – your people have to be just as bought in on what it's going to take to grow. You want a team that's locked into helping solve all the problems your organization has and your vision has to be so large that they can see themselves in it. You'll find that you've unlocked all of their mindshare. They'll be solving problems on your behalf, instead of you constantly having to solve them. If you are smart enough to put real incentives in front of somebody, success for everybody comes clearer.

Your understanding how vital incentives are to duplicating yourself within your organization should be crystal clear. Create the right structure around Incentive Plans, and you create a magnet for the right people to show up to level up their leadership as they follow the path you've created for them. This is one of the core components of all great leaders who do great things in business – they step back to see how they can create the greatest incentives for their people to win. I challenge you to make your vision about more than just you and your desires. Value your people by rewarding them for their results and making the target clear. Confusion always creates failure.

*All the exclusive resources I mention in the book are ready for you to use, along with videos, tools, and extras that I couldn't share in this book, go to **StartTheWorkTools.com**.*

YOUR TEAM

- ☑ TEAM GOALS
- ☑ METRICS
- ☑ INCENTIVES
- ☑ 1:1'S
- ☐ THE CYCLE OF SCALING

CHAPTER 18

ONE-ON-ONES

I'm going to be honest with you – I don't look forward to one-on-ones with my team members. That might not be what you expected me to say as I'm constantly sharing the importance of investing into your team, but that doesn't mean that my one-on-ones are filled with happy, encouraging, bliss filled moments. Sometimes it works out that way – when there are life announcements to share, PPF goals accomplished, and promotions given. I do love those one-on-ones. But those are the trophy moments – not the reality of what the day-to-day looks like while we're playing the game of scaling your business. One-on-ones convinced that anyone who says they do look forward to it is a liar. I dread it because I know it's going to be difficult and it's going to be challenging – but I do it anyway. And I'm always thrilled I did afterwards. It's just like any other discipline practice in your life: it's challenging but rewarding when you stick with it.

The reality is that one-on-ones are normally filled with problems. They're the dedicated time I get with each of my individual team members to go over the most pressing work that they need me to help coach them through or make a decision on. It's almost 5 hours straight of reviewing item after item with every one of my direct reports. Ideally no more than 8-12 people are reporting directly to you at any given time – and as I explain the one-on-ones process in this chapter, you'll understand why you should limit how many people report directly to you.

Before just diving into the process of how to structure your one-on-ones, it's important for me to point out that this time that you're spending with your team members is your duplication strategy – whether you acknowledge it or not. This is the dedicated time you have with the people you depend on, the people you're coaching, the people you are scaling through, to give them feedback and help them truly be high performers. Because of this, one-on-ones should always be in the Continue column in your Duplication Activity. And before you start pushing back on me, believe me, I understand how much you likely don't want to invest this time. I've had the same thoughts. "Maybe I could do group one-on-ones? What about doing them monthly or quarterly? How about I make them a 10-minute touch base? Now's not a good time – can't I push them off?" The answer is no. These are the most vital moments in the process of duplicating yourself in your business.

I think of it like this: If it's my job to be a coach, I need time with my individual team members to share with them what's working, what's not, and ensure they're on the same page. If I can't dedicate 1 hour each month to each of my team members, how effective of a coach can I really be? It's 60 minutes a month. That's it. In the scheme of things, that's not a lot of time. So you have to be incredibly intentional about ensuring it's used effectively and structured to hit on all of the different current and future opportunities that exist for their development.

One-on-ones are not the sexiest topic, but it's a serious topic when it comes to duplication and making effective use of your time. Now, as a leader, there is crucial cultural and operational information to be gleaned from these conversations, from important business Metrics pertaining to their specific role, to their personal, professional, and financial goals, their development plan, and so much more. Isn't it worth your time to develop a bond and support their growth if it means that you're creating a high-performing team in the process? You don't just want anyone doing this job, right? You want your employees to be the best, because ultimately their performance in their respective roles is what creates effectiveness allowing you to duplicate yourself and your processes.

But what is more important than simply conducting these meetings is conducting them in the right way. They're the key to shedding light on what you can plan to Start, Continue, Delegate, and/or Stop because you'll get real-time insight into your team's progress. Magic starts to happen when you roll out the Duplication Activity to your team members so they can embark on the same journey you've been on. This is inevitable as your team grows. They, like you, will have too many things and too little time. Use the one-on-ones to help your team assess where the best use of their time is spent so they can start their process of duplication and expanding their team.

THE PROCESS

No matter what size your business currently is, you should be conducting these meetings (as you are other aspects of the business) with your Vision statement in mind. Where do you intend to be ten years from now? Conduct and document your one-on-one meetings with that business in mind.

One-on-ones should be scheduled biweekly. I like to batch mine in thirty-minute increments every other Thursday. Having them back-to-back allows me to block off that time to solely focus on my primary role with my team: being a coach. When they are sprinkled throughout the week, it's easy to become transactional in your communication. I want these meetings to be fruitful, and the best way to set this up for success is batching them together. I place a recurring reminder the day before on my direct reports' calendars to send me their completed one-on-one forms. This gives me time to review them the following morning and get prepared for the conversation. I spend about thirty minutes reviewing them and making my own notes for areas I'd like to address. Earlier in my career, I didn't have this structure in place, and the one-on-ones were all over the place. They became more of a social function with an emphasis on "catching up". I never knew how to redirect the conversation to the business initiatives, but that changed as soon as I introduced these forms. I've used this template for over five years now and have helped thousands of businesses roll out this same structure for their meetings: it works like magic.

These are the essential areas you should cover in your one-on-ones.

ACTIONS TAKEN

Before moving onto new items, I start every one-on-one with reviewing the work that's taken place since our last meeting. It's incredibly frustrating to have a meeting where clear action items were established yet no progress was made afterward to complete them. This section should tie out to the previous one-on-one's "Action Plan" items. This is one way I reinforce our Core Values of Discipline and Accountability. If a team member says they will do something and don't, I have to address it in this meeting. One definition of leadership is one's ability to give and enforce orders. That can come across harshly, especially to new managers, but it's critical that you create a culture where leaders can establish what needs to get done and enforce that it actually happens. Without enforcing it, the environment becomes relaxed, and you'll sit back wondering why goals aren't being achieved.

METRICS

It's not by accident that the first order of business is reviewing each team member's Metrics. This is one way

I reiterate our Core Value of Results. Effort is great, but I need to know how each person is performing relative to already established expectations. If they're falling short, what actions are they taking to rectify that? This brings up two scenarios: First, what if the role doesn't have Metrics? Create them! There is no time like the present to button up the Metrics of every role inside your organization. The one-on-one meeting cadence with your team members holds you accountable for ensuring that Metrics do get created and are regularly reviewed. As discussed in the previous chapters, you are paying hourly for each contributor in your business, and when you hired them, there were specific business needs that drove you to make the post and find talent to help you. Every role should have clearly defined Metrics that they have visibility into. By implementing this one-on-one process, you're making the commitment to your team and yourself that you're going to get the business organized and provide clarity to each team member so they can create success. You will be amazed at how quickly this transforms your culture.

UPDATES AND IDEAS

This is one of my favorite sections of the one-on-one because it tells you a lot about where the employee's head is. If they don't have any ideas, this is a problem. Like all businesses, I'm certain that your business has growth opportunities. I've never worked with a perfectly dialed-in business where everything worked flawlessly. There are always areas that can be improved. This spot in the form is your team member's chance to identify the areas of opportunity that pertain to their role/ department. This section should be more informal, but request that they prioritize these ideas and make certain that these ideas about organizational improvement actually pertain to their department—otherwise, you're just throwing work into someone else's lap! I used to have these meetings, and by the end of them, I had a laundry list of items the team member put on my plate. This no longer happens. Sure, there are items that come up in this section that I end up needing to follow up on, but the majority of the time is spent with me approving new ideas and giving feedback on existing projects that are in the works. It's critically important for you to view yourself as a coach here. A coach doesn't run laps with the team. A coach is responsible for looking at the big picture, understanding the competition, and leveraging their experience to call the play. Stay focused on this as you go through this section.

PPF GOAL REVIEW

As I shared in Chapter 15, the one-on-one is the place where the team member is sharing updates on their goals. They might not have an update for every meeting, but there should be an area where they are identifying wins or setbacks across their goals. This conversation should be led by the team member and guided by the manager. This space creates the opportunity to continue conversations as goals change, developments are made, and wins occur. It's important to get visibility into these areas with your top performers as they will need specific coaching on how to get to the next level.

DEVELOPMENT PLAN

In my book *TeamWork*, I dive into how the Development Plan is created during the Performance Review process, but it's important to note here that this is how you create focus on long-term behavior development and change. This should include four to six areas where the team member can improve their professional performance over the course of the year. Many team members I've worked with have the desire to become better at public speaking because they recognize that their lack of confidence in this area holds them back from leadership opportunities. Well, something like public speaking skills doesn't just happen overnight. It requires intentionality over a period of time to improve. These areas are addressed here in the Development Plan of the one-on-one. The team member uses this portion of their one-on-one to share with their manager what steps they are taking and where there's improvement. If they aren't taking any steps in these areas, it's the manager's job to call attention to this and frame why it's important to continue to stay focused in these areas.

ACTION PLAN

This section is a takeaway for them to work on before your next meeting. They need to answer the question, "What are the steps and actions I will take after this meeting?" These are all the things that the team member documents and commits to so that when you next meet, they can answer the question, "What actions have you taken since our last one-on-one?"

The one-on-one structure creates accountability for your leaders to be coaches and your team members to be accountable to the outcome for their role. The accountability starts with the team member remembering to send the form ahead of the meeting. You both deserve the opportunity to prepare for this. No surprises. This is why we don't do these weekly at Cardone Ventures. It gives everyone a chance to take feedback, work to create a new result, and then report back on progress made.

Though I have been able to have a successful seventeen-minute One-on-One meeting, I recommend thirty minutes as a standard. Be very intentional about your time. It can go quickly. These team members have chosen your organization to grow their careers. Be focused and be constructive in your feedback. Hold them accountable to their word. And make tough decisions if they don't.

From an HR standpoint, this agenda allows you to document when you're working with an employee who is missing one of their Metrics so that if a termination does need to occur, you have this series of events in black and white. This protects the organization. And it's not all for negative circumstances. Documentation is equally important for positive business and performance outcomes and Incentives. In fact, it reinforces the kind of culture that you want to create.

It's taken me years to perfect this process but I haven't made a change to this outline since starting Cardone Ventures 5 years ago. It's helped me build great teams and a more successful business because it gets very specific about individual performance and accountability, which not only fosters great results, but also protects the integrity of your organization in the long run.

This level of integrity is essential as the glue that holds the structure of your Duplication process together. This small yet potent investment of time and effort on your part will have an exponential payout because it does a lot of the heavy lifting for you. This means you'll have your finger on the pulse of your culture, and your team, so you can quickly identify areas to pass on, to continue pursuing, to stop all together, and to start doing more of. For example, if you're conducting a one-on-one with a team member and you look at their Updates and Ideas, this may flip a switch for you to develop a process they can take over for you or another leader. This empowers that person, clears room on your plate, and creates new opportunities you wouldn't have known about otherwise, saving you time in the process.

These brief, essential, and powerful meetings provide feedback from boots on the ground level to help you continue to fuel the upward momentum within the cycle of scaling.

*All the exclusive resources I mention in the book are ready for you to use, along with videos, tools, and extras that I couldn't share in this book, go to **StartTheWorkTools.com**.*

YOUR
TEAM

CHAPTER 19

THE CYCLE OF SCALING

I recently stumbled upon a journal of mine from 2020. Curious, I opened it up for a trip down memory lane. The entry that stood out to me the most was the one from when we had just hit $1 million a month in revenue at Cardone Ventures.

We were freaking out. This was an achievement I had dreamed of for a long time. Reaching that mark was trilling, astonishing, and validating all at once. Every single little thing we had put into our business, all the moments we had spent plugging away, these all had built into that million dollar figure. But it did not stop there – and the four years since have been a process of discovering, testing, and developing the scaling tools and practices you've now learned about in this book.

Just a few months ago in our Annual Planning Meeting, we announced to the team that we had generated over $146 million in annual revenue in 2023. This was a real "pinch me" moment. There are certainly levels to this game of business. Somewhat surprisingly, initially hitting the $1 million mark was just as exciting as the $146 million that was to come. For those who continue to grow their business, achievement first and foremost represents proof that you can go out and reach the next marker you set for yourself. You could be on your first 7 figures or closing your first sale. What changes the further you go along is your confidence in what you're capable of achieving. When you generate your first million dollars, there's still doubt that can undercut your sense of accomplishment. You may feel like you got lucky, that great year of business was the product of coincidence, or it was all one freak accident that's about to crumble like a house of cards.

As you advance, you're able to ditch these insecurities and take pride in your ability to consistently create growth. When you follow the process for scaling as we've discussed in this book, there is no such thing as luck and your growth is no fluke. You're not flying by the seat of your pants, not anymore at least. You're climbing the ladder and duplicating yourself each step of the way. It's great to reflect on these accomplishments. But I want to remind you that it's not all exciting year end meetings and ecstatic journal entries about "pinch-me" moments.

The tools that are explored in this book are not meant to be just used once. I used them to generate our first million in revenue – and I'll use them time and again until we've hit our target of impacting the lives of 1 million business owners. My hope is that you're able to say the same. As you scale and you find yourself stuck, I want you to be able to turn to this book as a handbook filled with ways to keep moving onwards and upwards towards your business goals. This isn't a book about getting to a destination. It's the practices that will help you thrive in the perpetual journey that is scaling a business. Some people may find this frustrating. It's like mowing the lawn. No matter how well you do it, you will have to cut the grass again next week. Right when you've achieved your business' revenue and profitability goals, you find yourself back at it to start another year with a new set of goals.

You may have gotten into business with the idea that one day, like a stoic Clint Eastwood, you'd ride off into the sunset with a bag of cash. Or maybe there's an image of you sipping drinks on the beach and living happily ever after. These moments are short lived, the joy is in continuously asking yourself "What is my potential?"

In 2016, I had the unique experience of watching my now husband sell his business for the amount that he always dreamed of: $155 million. He built the business from the ground up with that one goal in mind and achieved it. Two months later, he was unhappy, and thinking about the next, even bigger thing. The life lesson I got from seeing that? If you have this thing inside you that wants to build – and you believe you can impact people – there is no endgame or final target.

Sometimes it can feel like you're running on a hamster wheel. Maintaining the passion and remembering the excitement during the grind is a daily thing. Every day, I book in what I call a "Daily Success Meeting" with myself. It's a three minute time slot, usually before we kick off team meetings, and it's time set aside for myself and my thoughts. It's there for me to remind myself of what I did successfully the day before. When you are playing this game, it's easy to feel like you're constantly failing. You're so focused on getting to the next thing that you forget the last goal you smashed out the park. Having these moments set aside will keep you focused on the greater mission at hand, as you go through each minute step to getting there.

I often ask myself: am I really that excited to wake up at five o'clock in the morning to answer emails? To counter this, I have to ensure there are things in my environment that remind me why I'm doing that. One of the things that's going to give your business rocket fuel is this: surrounding yourself with people who are looking to scale their lives to that potential, even when it gets difficult. At Cardone Ventures, we live by the motto that the number one rule of success is showing up. Even when I'm not feeling 10X, don't want to go into the next meeting, and sometimes don't feel like getting out of bed in the morning, I am reminded of the next place that I want to be – and know I can't get there if I don't at least walk into the door.

By reading this book, you have shown up for your business. Now is the time to start the work to scale your organization beyond what you used to think possible. Be intentional about reminding yourself of the impact that you can have on your team, clients, industry, and world. Nothing will keep the fire burning like that.

A year from now, when you're doing regular maintenance on your weekly schedule and sorting Start, Stop, Delegate, and Continue tasks like it's second nature, you'll be proud of the work you put in. The day to day of your business and your schedule will be changing by the week, but the theory underlying how your organization scales will remain familiar. You'll be able to use the last success to reinforce your confidence for the next challenge ahead. Believe me, there are moments when I have to take a step back and remind myself to apply the tools you've learned in this book.

The problems don't go away. It doesn't matter how far your business has gone – all the fires, the messes, and the ugly parts of running an organization don't disappear. What does change is your ability to handle them, the amount of people around you to tackle them, and the resources you have to throw at them. So if you're always going to have these problems, why not just make your business so large that you have hundreds, if not thousands, of people helping you?

We'll leave our friend Sarah Scales to continue growing her business. That real estate she checked out is now a fully-loaded dental clinic getting ready for its grand opening. Managing the development of her hygienists is as easy as opening a spreadsheet with their Metrics and training using the Tell Me, Show Me, Let Me, Coach Me

Onboarding Plan. Sure, Sarah might miss the one-on-one time with patients, but the anecdotes and jokes she used to tell them translate well to the instructional dental hygiene videos she's posting on social media to promote the business.

Not only has Sarah recognized that working *on* her business is different than working *in* her business, she's also started the work. Sarah's somebody we all can strive to be, though sometimes we may feel like we're running our own business like Sean Stagnates. The good news about Sean is this: his biggest problem was what he didn't know. He understood how to work in his business, but was never taught what it looks like to work on his business. He was flying by the seat of his pants, until he cracked open this book. Now, there are no excuses. He has the tools, the strategies, and the processes for not just creating scale, but replicating growth time and again. From his own skillset and mindset, to the way he manages his team, to the way that he interfaces with patients, he has discovered how to duplicate what's already working. This has freed up the time he now uses to reveal new avenues that work even better. Sean's rolling up his sleeves – all fired up about what can be made possible.

I'm in the same boat as you. When I finish this book, I'm going right back to applying the tools and methods within it to continue scaling my business. What are you waiting for? You know what to do, now Start The Work.

*All the exclusive resources I mention in the book are ready for you to use, along with videos, tools, and extras that I couldn't share in this book, go to **StartTheWorkTools.com.***

CONCLUSION

WHAT'S NEXT?

Now it's your time to implement. The greatest ideas in the world mean nothing without implementation. No matter where you're at in your business lifecycle, it is never too early or too late to develop a process for aligning, developing, and transitioning your team.

Milton Keynes UK
Ingram Content Group UK Ltd.
UKHW021343230924
1801UKWH00012B/20/J

9 798218 428822